Writing Winning Business Plans

*How to Prepare a Business Plan
that Investors will Want to Read
– and Invest In*

GARRETT SUTTON, ESQ.

Writing Winning Business Plans

How to Prepare a Business Plan
that Investors will Want to Read
– and Invest In

GARRETT SUTTON, ESQ.

BZK
PRESS

Published by BZK Press, LLC

Rich Dad Advisors, B-I Triangle, CASHFLOW Quadrant and other Rich Dad marks are registered trademarks of CASHFLOW Technologies, Inc.

BZK Press LLC
2248 Meridian Blvd.
Suite H
Minden, NV 89423
775-782-2201
Visit our Web sites: BZKPress.com and RichDadAdvisors.com

Printed in the United States of America

First Edition: July 2005
First BZK Press Edition: April 2012

ISBN: 978-1-937832-01-8

Acknowledgments

I would like to acknowledge Mona Gambetta and Brandi MacLeod for their assistance in revising and updating this book from the original *"ABC's of Writing Winning Business Plans,"* first published in 2005. I would also like to thank my wife, Jenny, and children, Teddy, Emily and Sarah, for their continued patience as these books are being revised and updated.

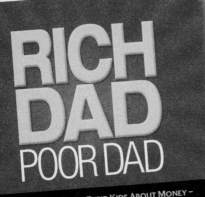

Best-Selling Books
In the Rich Dad Advisors Series

by Blair Singer

SalesDogs
You Don't Have to Be an Attack Dog to Explode Your Income

Team Code of Honor
The Secrets of Champions in Business and in Life

by Garrett Sutton, Esq.

Start Your Own Corporation
Why the Rich Own their Own Companies and Everyone Else Works for Them

Writing Winning Business Plans
*How to Prepare a Business Plan that Investors will Want to Read –
and Invest In*

Buying and Selling a Business
How You Can Win in the Business Quadrant

The ABCs of Getting Out of Debt
Turn Bad Debt into Good Debt and Bad Credit into Good Credit

Run Your Own Corporation
*How to Legally Operate and Properly Maintain Your Company
into the Future*

by Ken McElroy

The ABCs of Real Estate Investing

The Secrets of Finding Hidden Profits Most Investors Miss

The ABCs of Property Management
What You Need to Know to Maximize Your Money Now

The Advanced Guide to Real Estate Investing
How to Identify the Hottest Markets and Secure the Best Deals

by Tom Wheelwright

Tax-Free Wealth
*How to Build Massive Wealth by **Permanently** Lowering Your Taxes*

by Andy Tanner

Stock Market Cash Flow
Four Pillars of Investing for Thriving in Today's Markets

by Josh and Lisa Lannon

The Social Capitalist
Entrepreneurs' Journeys from Passion to Profits

by Wayne Palmer

Recipes for Real Estate
100 Formulas for Real Estate Riches

Contents

Foreword
by Robert Kiyosaki

When I left the Marines I had to decide which father's advice to follow. My real father, my poor dad, wanted me to go back to school and get a good job with a big corporation so I could "climb the corporate ladder" as an employee. My best friend's father, my rich dad, advised me to "build my own corporate ladder" as an entrepreneur. But he also told me that if I wanted to become an entrepreneur I first had to learn how to sell. So I joined Xerox for the sole purpose of learning to sell. I had decided that I was going to become an entrepreneur.

When I was ready to make the leap from employee to entrepreneur, I had already become the top salesperson for Xerox. I was even more committed to becoming an entrepreneur because I had realized that I did not want to work harder and harder for the next thirty years to make someone else rich. I wanted to work less and less to make more and more to make myself rich and pay less in taxes, just like my rich dad taught me. When I went to tell him the great news, he bluntly asked me one question, "Are you willing to pay the price?"

What kind of question was that? I thought. Of course I was willing to pay the price. I had just become a top salesperson for a major corporation just as he had told me to do. Think about what I could accomplish selling products I myself had created and had great passion for. I was ready, or so I thought.

So I threw myself into creating a nylon-and-Velcro surfer wallet company with two partners. Starting out, it was a great ride. We developed new products that quickly generated millions of dollars worth of orders.

We were millionaires and felt like we had conquered the world. Cash was rolling in and the future looked bright. We were at the top of our game when we went to the Sporting Goods Trade Show in Los Angeles in 1978. We arrived at the show very confident and excited about our prospects. That excitement came to a screeching halt. We were shocked to find that competitor after competitor was flooding the market with *our* products. I was determined to stop them from ripping off my ideas. The problem was I couldn't. I had not legally protected my product because I had thought getting a patent was too expensive. My first big business was out of business in less than a year, and we were deeply in debt.

I had wanted immediate success. Who needs to take the time to gain practical experience? Who needs to work tirelessly for months on end to research and write a winning business plan with a competent team of advisors? Dreams and intense determination were going to be my keys to success. I was beginning to better understand rich dad's question, "Are you willing to pay the price?"

You know the old saying, "If I only knew then what I know now." When rich dad learned of my company's fate he simply smiled and said, "Failing to plan is planning to fail." Then he added, "Failing is part of winning. This means you are one step closer to winning. Keep going."

Money Follows Great Entrepreneurs

Investors like winners, and that means money follows great entrepreneurs. The better track record you have, the easier it will be to raise money for your business. On the other hand, many good business plans don't attract money – not because of the deal but because of the people controlling the deal.

There are a lot of people chasing dollars to start a new business or launch a new product. The biggest problem most of them have is that they personally lack experience or they have no team behind them, or they have a team that doesn't inspire confidence. If the team is weak or lacks experience and a track record, I rarely invest.

My rich dad taught me that true entrepreneurs love building businesses for the challenge of it. They start new companies because they can't imagine doing anything else. They know that each new business plan has a price and they are willing to pay it, no matter how large – and they have a track record of success to prove it.

Start Small and Build

I recommend that people start small and build, leveraging other people's training programs and systems to gain the experience, education, team of advisors, and track record of success to move on to "Big Deals" like the ones on our board game CASHFLOW. A great way to start small and build is to pursue opportunities in franchising or network marketing, because these provide great training and proven systems. Starting a part-time business while you are still an employee can help reduce the stress of "needing a paycheck" while you create your business plan.

I Invest First in People!

As a sophisticated investor, I know to invest in people. I look for spirited entrepreneurs who are prepared to succeed and are "willing to pay the price." They've done their homework and have a strong track record of success. The better they are at basics, the more money they will make me with less risk. Building a business may be the riskiest road for most people. But if you can survive and keep improving your skills, your potential for wealth is unlimited. If you avoid risk and play it safe, you may limit what you can earn and find yourself in a dead-end job.

In *Writing Winning Business Plans*, Rich Dad Advisor Garrett Sutton outlines the specific "how-to" of writing a winning business plan by combining practical advice with "street-smart" rich dad principles. Garrett not only provides a framework to write your plan, he forces you to think differently and encourages you to ask the tough questions that, if answered honestly, can improve the odds for your business. If you are ready to dare to live your dreams, this book is for you.

Remember that the primary goal of a winning business plan is to have investors lined up to give you money. This book will help you write the plan that investors WANT you to read.

Thank you.
Robert Kiyosaki

Chapter One

Plan to Win

"Winning isn't everything, but wanting to win is."
– Vince Lombardi

Congratulations on making the decision to turn your dream into a business plan. It's an exciting step and you are to be commended. Most people's fear of failure and inability to take risks are stronger than their desire to live their dreams. That's fine for them, but it limits their lives.

Now that you have made the choice to go from an idea to a plan, the goal of this book is to both provide a framework for winning business plans and more importantly, to challenge your thinking. There is a standard format that virtually all business plans adhere to. Rather than simply providing yet another rehash of the standard format, we will combine the basic "how-to's" with tough questions and street-smart insights into what savvy investors and lenders are really looking for in each section of your plan.

Successful entrepreneurs naturally embrace the challenge of making their dream a reality. Creating a new business is exciting, challenging and requires all of you to make it successful. By learning to build a successful business those with true entrepreneurial spirit will develop a profession few will ever achieve.

Remember though that nine out of ten new businesses fail despite plans that communicate great opportunity. In reality, most businesses fail not because of poorly written business plans, they lose because their owners don't prepare themselves for the real world of business. So before we begin the "how-to" section of this book, it's critical that you answer two key questions:

1) How bad do you want to win?

This is the first question to ask yourself as you begin the journey of turning your dream into a winning business plan. If your inner-drive and motivation to start a business aren't big enough, the "how-to" of a plan doesn't matter.

2) Are you mentally prepared to own your own business?

Dreams are romantic gestures that provide great inspiration. With a business plan, inspiration meets perspiration. Starting your own business will take everything you have. The common theme in all novice business plans in an underestimation of the time, energy, experience and money necessary to build a winning business.

Each business plan has a price. Most people want successful businesses but are not willing to first invest the time. They want get rich quick schemes and often start businesses without basic skills. Most people do it "their way" instead of investing in study and building a team of competent advisors.

Great business plans come from entrepreneurs willing to delay immediate gratification. They take risks and invest the time and energy necessary to gain relevant experience and education. They are not afraid of making mistakes or failing because mistakes and failure equal experience. They start small and build, recognizing experience leads to greater ability. After paying the price, true entrepreneurs gain the knowledge to build a winning plan and winning business.

Most business plans are written to attract funding to start a business or expand an existing business. Plans are also written to help existing businesses grow, but that aspect of "strategic planning" is different than the focus of this book, which is to provide a framework to convince an investor, and yourself, that your plan possesses the necessary ingredients to become one of the 5% of new businesses that succeed. Savvy investors and lenders know the odds and unless you educate yourself on the realities of winning plans, your plan will likely make its way to the bottom of the waste basket.

Business is a plan, not a product or procedure. Good plans expect the unexpected, but remain intact and in use throughout the trying early years. They just keep getting improved upon as you learn more. Your personal plan can be financial freedom—freedom from the day to day grind of working for money. But your business plan has to answer the following questions for investors and lenders:

1. Can I make money investing in this business (risk vs. reward)?
2. Do I like and understand the business I'm investing in?
3. Do I trust the people I am investing with?

It's also important to note that winning in business has much more to do with entrepreneurial spirit than it does with age or gender. You're never too old or too young to be a successful entrepreneur. In *Rich Dad's Guide to Investing*, Robert Kiyosaki describes the personal traits of a successful entrepreneur:

1) Vision: Ability to find opportunities others cannot see

2) Courage: Ability to act despite tremendous doubt

3) Creativity: Ability to think outside the box

4) Ability to withstand criticism: There is not one successful person who has not been criticized

5) Ability to delay gratification: It can be very difficult to learn to deny short-term immediate self-gratification in favor of a greater long-term reward

So as you begin to write your plan, ask yourself if you truly have the tenacity to fail and start the challenge again. Nearly all successful entrepreneurs have had many failures. The beautiful thing about business is that you don't have to be right 51% of the time, you only have to be right once.

Rich Dad Tips

- As you begin the process of creating a new business surround yourself with successful and like-minded people

- Take the time to really think about what you want in this gift called your life. Many new businesses owners have a dream of freedom and end up creating a "job" for themselves.

- Don't forget to plan your exit at the beginning. Too many people get caught up in starting a business and fail to think about preparing for its end goal.

- There is never a perfect time to start a business. If you want to live your dream, prepare yourself as well as you possibly can and then take action!

Chapter Two

Why Do You Need a Plan?

"By failing to prepare, you are preparing to fail."
– Benjamin Franklin

Writing a winning business plan is necessary whether you need outside investors or not. The process of writing a winning plan forces you to invest significant time and energy into thinking about your business and doing your homework. Consider the case of new business owners, one without a plan and one with a plan...

Fred and Ted

Fred and Ted are competitive friends. Their friendship was based on a never ending quest to determine who could do athletic activities, brainteasers or whatever competition came to mind the fastest, the longest or by whatever winning standard they came up with.

Fred and Ted were both single and just about to finish college. The last three summers they had worked together for Max's Lawns, a local lawn mowing service. They both liked the business and both unconsciously realized that due to their competitive streaks, they couldn't co-own a lawn service together. This was certified when their girlfriends refused to double date due to their adolescent competitive behavior. In no uncertain terms both women agreed they'd be doomed if they ever went in business together. They both privately knew that their girlfriend's intuition was spot on.

With college graduation approaching and no real prospects each decided to start their own lawn mowing/snow removal service.

Fred was first out of the starting gate. He had learned enough from Max's Lawns to get started. You needed a truck, some equipment and plenty of flyers to announce your new introductory discount prices.

Ted was more cautious. He decided to stay on with Max's for the summer to learn even more about the business. He bought and read books on how to start and operate a lawn care/snow removal business. He spent time analyzing the local market to see where the price points were. He learned that by discounting at the start of operations you may always be seen as a discount provider. He learned that the low end of the market place is not always the best place to be.

Ted went to business classes put on by the local SCORE* group and asked questions about incorporating and workmen's compensation issues. He sought out the help of his uncle's friend, who had run his own lawn mowing/snow removal service for nearly thirty years before retiring. He took in all the information he obtained and began to formalize it into a cohesive business plan.

Ted and Fred got together for darts and beer in late July. Fred was crowing about how well his business was going. He had borrowed $20,000 from his Dad to get it started. He now had twenty new clients on his discount, introductory plan. He and a co-worker were busy. Ted asked him how much his workmen's compensation costs were running him. Fred drew a blank. Ted explained the need for workmen's compensation on your employees in case they get injured on the job. Fred said he would look into it. Fred, ever competitive, chided Ted on how long he would stay with Max. Ted replied until he was ready. As Fred left that night he felt the victor in this competition. For his part, Ted sensed the benefit of developing a plan and implementing it when he was ready.

---

* Service Corp of Retired Executives, a part of the Small Business Administration (www.score.org)

Two months later Ted and Fred ran into each other. Ted asked Fred how the business was going. Fred was dejected. His worker had been severely injured on the job. He didn't have workmen's compensation coverage on the employee. So the worker's attorney was suing both he and the homeowner to cover the large medical bills. The homeowner was furious at being sued, and was now suing Fred for indemnification. The homeowner was also telling all of Fred's other clients that Fred was without coverage. They were canceling their contracts. Worse yet, Fred had failed to incorporate so now all his personal assets, meager as they were, were exposed to the worker's claims. He was nearing bankruptcy, which would prevent him from getting back into business for an uncertain amount of time.

Ted was sympathetic to Fred's plight. But it served to further remind him of the benefits of planning instead of running head long into doing. He had learned that a business plan is not only a road map, but a checklist of things that must be done in their proper order. A checklist is found in Appendix "A". By analyzing and planning, Ted had learned the importance and the risks of failing to incorporate and obtain insurance coverage. By going step by step through the business plan process he was alerted to many different types of business risks before he got into business.

What did Ted and Fred learn?

Fred didn't plan to win. Even though taking action is the most important part of starting a new business, failing to educate yourself on at least the basics of owning a business in a particular field forced him to painfully gain a real world education of what happens when you don't do your homework.

Ted plans to win, so he began by first preparing himself to be a business owner. He kept a job not for the paycheck, but for what he could learn, and he surrounded himself with advisors who had experience and a track record of success. Which of the two would you invest in?

Let's take a look at Rich Dad's Cashflow Quadrant to explain how Fred is operating in the "S" or self-employed quadrant and Ted is operating in the "B" or business quadrant. People in the "S" quadrant want to do things their way (solo players). They believe they are the only people with the ability to get the job done. They often achieve strong early results and then come to the painful realization that rather than the business of their dreams they actually created a job for themselves. By building a business that relies solely on their time and ability, people in "S" quadrant cannot remove themselves from their business without losing cash flow. The only way to grow is to personally work more and more. This difficult trap could have been avoided if they would have planned differently at the beginning and led differently during the creation of the business.

People in the "B-quadrant" want to work less and less to make more and more. Like the "S-quadrant" person, they typically work very hard during the early stages of a business, but they work on very different things than someone in the "S" quadrant. They focus on creating assets that deliver passive cash flow or can be sold. "B-quadrant" people build teams of employees, advisors and mentors that grow businesses without them (team players).

As you begin formulating your winning plan, be wary of some of the common traps new entrepreneurs fall into:

Trap #1: Failing to plan is planning to fail

Effective planning means more than writing goals on a piece of paper. It means taking personal responsibility to prepare you emotionally and practically to be a business owner. Unrealistic assumptions and poorly written plans communicate a lack of preparation to investors.

Trap #2: Plan your exit--do you want a business or a job?

Many novice entrepreneurs create businesses that become their jobs rather than provide the freedom and passive income they dreamed of. As a result of poor planning, many new businesses generate little to no cash flow and require the full time effort of the owner. If your dream is to have both personal and financial freedom, plan to build a business that can at some point run itself and provide excessive cash flow. Recognize that it often takes many years of blood, sweat and tears to get to that point.

Trap #3: Many novices want to "do it their way"

By failing to educate themselves in the basics of operating a business, new entrepreneurs fail to surround themselves with a competent team of employees, advisors and mentors. They are solo players instead of team players.

Trap #4: A winning business plan is not an academic exercise

Many businesses fail despite having beautifully written plans complete with optimistic projections. A business plan is not a school term paper. Yes, to get your plan read it needs to be virtually perfect in appearance, format, layout and grammar. Unfortunately, in the real world, earning an "A" in appearance and forgetting to emphasize the thought and substance of a plan often results in an "F" in the area that matters most—a business with excessive cash flow that serves a purpose greater than money.

Trap #5: I have the best product!

The world is full of great products and short of great entrepreneurs. Successful businesses require great people first, great systems second and great products third. Think about companies like Microsoft (Bill Gates), Dell Computer (Michael Dell) and McDonald's (Ray Kroc). Their success is a result of the passion of their entrepreneurs and the uniqueness of the business systems they created. In many cases, wildly successful companies have products that are high quality but not the best in the market. They achieve their growth because they have superior people and business systems with sustainable and unique advantages.

Rich Dad Tips

- A great product doesn't make a business successful. Great people make a business successful.

- The problem with being a solo player is that you are individual competing against a team.

- If you're the smartest person on your team, your team may be in trouble

Chapter Three

Business Plan Basics

"We live in an age of haste. Some people look at an egg and expect it to crow."
– Orison S. Marden

You may be in a hurry to put together your business plan. But don't confuse the frenetic blur of activity with thoughtful preparation. There are some major issues to discuss in your plan, and you've got to think them through.

Winning business plans map out the major W's of your proposed business -- who, what, when, why and where -- to help you figure out that all important H -- how. Who are the major players? Who are the owners, personnel, advisors, customers, competition, even the target audience for the plan itself? What do you want to achieve? What is your sustainable advantage? What do you offer? What do you produce? When did (will) the business start? When do you want to meet particular goals? Why are you in business? Why would customers want your product or service? Where is the business located? Where is the target audience? Where do new opportunities lie? And finally, how do you get from where you are now to where you want to be?

Rich Dad Tips

- Money follows management. Investors typically look first at the people involved in the company. The experience, education and track record of management and advisors need to be given great emphasis.

Ideally, a business plan is the intersection of everything inside the business (costs, products, services, personnel, etc.) and everything outside the business (competition, market trends, political forces, etc). Forces inside the company meet those outside the company and a business plan is born.

Many entrepreneurs put too much emphasis on the inside forces and ignore the outside. No business is an island; no company operates in a vacuum. Even as you are tackling all the tiny details that need to be included in your plan, be sure to keep a grip on the big picture.

A winning business plan outlines goals, clearly communicates strategies and establishes plans for both the best and worst case scenarios (as well as any and all scenarios in between) that might befall your company. Seasoned entrepreneurs and investors know to expect the unexpected and at the same time anticipate the challenges inherent in each particular business.

In great business plans, you not only sell your business concept, you sell yourself. Your entrepreneurial spirit and passion are critical factors to a potential investor. Communicating your team's experience, abilities and track record will take you even farther. The key is showing how your experience and abilities will support your business and help it to excel.

Rich Dad Tips

- Seasoned investors aren't fooled by "hyped" words hastily written to compensate for a lack of experience or education. If you are starting out and don't have relevant experience, it's best to show that you are surrounding yourself with an experienced team of advisors and employees. Business is a team sport.

A good business plan can help you determine what you need to make your business a success -- from personnel to financing, location to advertising. But to truly make your company succeed, you must pay attention to what you find during plan preparation. Be thoughtful. Don't do the plan, figure out you need $300,000 and then try to wing it on $150,000. Be realistic in your planning, then be just as realistic in following the plan.

The hardest part of crafting a good business plan (or even a bad one, for that matter) is overcoming inertia. Most people have a great idea and fail to take action because of a fear of failure. A body at rest tends to stay at rest; a body in motion tends to stay in motion. Inertia is what keeps a body at rest (along with a comfy couch, a good TV night, high-speed internet service, whatever). Kick inertia in its thermodynamic behind, get off your couch and get started. Now. Don't wait until you finish this book. Don't even wait until you finish this chapter. Go now and grab a pen and a notebook and start taking notes. Sometimes the simple motion of moving a pen across a page is enough to get the rest of your body in motion.

Just as you must overcome inertia to construct a business plan, you might also have to overcome fear. A business plan sounds complicated. But it shouldn't be. A complicated business plan is often worse than no business plan at all. Your plan should be understandable in its language (overly technical terms that confuse are not welcome); it should summarize where appropriate (leave the details for appendices); and it should truly describe your business (leave the boilerplates for metal shop). It needs to be short and to the point. Keep it simple, but make it complete. Treat your plan as if it is the only information a potential investor, lender or manager will have before making a decision enabling the success of your business.

Writing a business plan is a labor of love, but also an exercise in logic and forethought. Embarking on the task of planning on paper what will likely consume your life and should serve several critical functions:

1. A business plan helps you clarify, focus and research your business' development and prospects. Now, keep in mind that planning does not mean predicting the future (crystal balls are not required), but rather it means being aware of a wide range of likely futures and being prepared for them as they occur. Try to imagine the questions you might have if you were a shareholder, investor or representative of a financial institution. You will need to be able to succinctly explain the purpose of your plan (let alone the business); the vision, goals and strategies you have for your business; and any achievements and/or performances you have had to date (think financial, sales and technical). You will need to describe your product(s) or services in relation to the market and industry as a whole.

2. A business plan provides the framework to create a company's mission, goals and key strategies. In addition to explaining each of these in great detail, this book we will insert "street smart" principles from Rich Dad's B-I Triangle into relevant sections.

The B-I Triangle's foundation is a company's mission, team and leadership. Its primary elements are cash flow, communications, systems, legal and product. For a complete explanation of the B-I Triangle, read *Rich Dad's Guide To Investing* by Robert Kiyosaki.

3. A business plan can serve as a basis for discussion with third parties, such as shareholders, agencies, banks, investors and the like. Mapping out the financial position and projections for your business should be used to get funds, whether your company is established or just in the startup phase. Most banks and lenders will need to have at least the basics of your business on paper in order to discuss the merits of your business or idea. Most must report to others (such as a loan committee) and won't want to take you along to talk over their shoulders. In order to develop a good, useable business plan, you must understand your business finances. Funding requirements, possible sources, likely terms and projected return on investments are all real concerns to investors and lenders, as they should be for you as well. So be sure to be

realistic. The temptation to exaggerate can be great, but resist. Back up your numbers with more numbers, with reasoning and with research. Though using a business plan as part of a request for funds is a legitimate use of a business plan, watch out for making this the only function. Your business plan is your road map to the future.

4. A business plan is a benchmark against which actual performance can be measured and reviewed. It allows you to quantitatively measure reality against goals. A business plan is an organic document, a perpetual work-in-progress. Comparing projections to actual numbers will help you measure performance and thereby give you what you need to keep your plan useful. Just as you don't want to fly blindly into a business, nor do you want to implement changes on a whim. A business plan will help you get started on the right foot and then keep you moving in the right direction.

There are as many outlines for business plans as there are business plans, with each of them being minor derivatives of each other. They are all basically the same and tend to be comprised of four standard segments:

1. The Business. Also called Business Strategy or Business Description, this section might include such subsections as Business Opportunity, Organization and Operations, Legal Structure, Business Model, Operating Procedures, Operations Description, Management, Personnel, Strengths and Weaknesses, Core Competencies and Challenges, Business Accomplishments, Location, Product Offering, Product or Service, Records and Insurance. By the time a reader completes this section, he or she should have a thorough and concrete understanding of your business. This section discusses all pertinent aspects of your business. It covers every aspect of production from idea to service after the sale, including the management, personnel, equipment, paperwork and property involved. For service businesses the product is the service.

Rich Dad Tips

- In the Business section, make sure you "sell" the one reason your business will be able to generate excessive cash flow. Remember that you are selling by communicating your experience and education, not by promoting your company with empty words and promises.

---

2. The Marketing. Also called Market Strategy and including subsections such as Target Markets, Customers, Competition, Distribution, Relationships, Advertising, Pricing, Industry and Market Trends, Strategy and Market Strategy. The Marketing section is a thorough discussion of the industry and your business' place in it. It covers all the forces that come to bear on your business. From the customers to the competition, advertising to pricing, industry trends to global economics, this section gives the reader a thorough understanding of how your business will deal with getting the product to potential buyers.

Rich Dad Tips

- A key pitfall of many novice entrepreneurs is not knowing how to "get the word out" on their business. Astute business owners understand how to leverage public relations, viral marketing through word of mouth and the internet to attract new customers.

- Traditional advertising is often expensive and inefficient. True entrepreneurs have a guerilla marketing spirit that allows them to achieve great value from minimal marketing investments.

---

3. The Financials. Also called Financial Data or The Deal and includes subsections such as Uses of Funds, Income Statements, Cash Flow Statement, Balance Sheet, Cash Flow Forecast, Profit and Loss Forecast, Income Projection, Sales Revenue Forecast, Income Forecast, Capital Spending Plan, Assumptions, Budget and Break-Even Analysis. The Financial section is all about the numbers. The past, present and future are all represented. You will include tables that lay out the money side of your business. Short-term and long-term costs and revenues are presented in ways that will help management and/or financial experts to determine the risk of your business idea.

Rich Dad Tips

- In their haste, novice entrepreneurs underestimate the time, energy and money required to build a successful business. They tend to underestimate costs and overestimate revenues and time to achieve them.

- Many savvy investors place little emphasis on the credibility of the numbers because everyone knows they are a guess. They are looked at primarily for an investor or lender to determine if they are in a range of reality.

- It's important to benchmark similar companies so you can show you have done your homework.

- If you don't have financial statement experience, this is an area where you must leverage an advisor or risk losing credibility.

4. The Supporting Material. The material used will depend upon the type of business for which you are planning as well as the contents of the rest of your plan. Common supporting documents include resumes, letters of reference, credit reports, legal documents, agreements and contracts. This is information that needs no textual introduction or explanation or that is introduced or explained in the previous sections of the plan.

In addition, most business plan have a separate cover sheet, a table of contents, an executive summary and some text introducing the business mission and goals, each of which averages one page.

For our purposes, we will use the following outline:

Cover Sheet
Table of Contents
Mission Statement
Executive Summary
The Business
Strengths and Weaknesses
       Legal Structure
       Business Description
       Product or Service Description
       Intellectual Property Description
       Location
       Management and Personnel
       Records
       Insurance
       Security
       Litigation
The Marketing
       Markets
       Competition
       Distribution and Sales
       Marketing

Although not necessarily in the exact order above, we shall discuss the various elements of the outline and how to flesh them out into a winning business plan in the chapters ahead. Some funding and/or investment entities may have their own outline to follow. If you are given guidelines, follow them. Remember the golden rule. Those with the gold get to make the rules.

Ideally, by the time the plan is complete, you will have enough information to suit anyone's guidelines. Compiling the initial information is the real work. Rearranging it into different formats should not be difficult. No matter what outline you choose, be sure to cover all your bases. It is tempting to skip management information if you are preparing the plan for loan purposes only or to skip financials if you are preparing the plan for your own management purposes. If you want to give into temptation, have a piece of chocolate. Do not let temptation shortchange all the potential usefulness of a business plan. You never know when having a complete business plan will, out of the blue, lead to a large opportunity. Be concise, but be thorough.

If there are no content requirements from lenders or investors, customize your plan to suit yourself and/or your management team. Consider the Rich Dad B-I Triangle as a useful format. Use headings that you and your team understand. For example, does "Core Competencies and Challenges" or "Strengths and Weaknesses" make more sense to you? Does your company deal with licenses rather than manufactured products? Then name and construct your sections accordingly. Ease of understanding is the cornerstone of any good business plan. Remember, there is no federal or state law mandating what has to be in a business plan. Obviously you can't make material misstatements or fraudulent claims, but beyond that caveat the content is up to you. So write it to satisfy the questions both a novice and a sophisticated investor would ask.

Before choosing what to include in each section and subsection of your plan, you may want to do some detailed outlining -- not necessarily to include in your plan, but for your own use. Know yourself so that you can build your plan to help you. If you know numbers are your weak point, spend some extra time coming to terms with the Financials section of your plan and surround yourself with experts and mentors. If you're a math whiz, but linear goal setting sets your teeth on edge, take some extra time to build planning sections. If you have someone else help you develop your plan (which is a great way to supplement your own areas of expertise), be sure you spend the time necessary to work closely with the planner on their section because it is your business and the plan must be a reflection of you.

If you are preparing your plan for a franchise startup, pay close attention to the manuals, materials and operating procedures provided to you by the franchisor. Read everything carefully before you begin to write your plan. This information is the starting point of your plan and much of it may be able to be incorporated directly into your plan. Take advantage of the experience of those who have traveled this path before you. And be careful that your plan is not so far removed from the franchisor's operations that your franchise becomes incompatible with the chain from which it came. Franchisers have strict guidelines they expect each franchisee to follow. We all know what happens to the nail that sticks out above the rest.

That said, business plans are beneficial to a number of businesses and activities that one wouldn't normally associate with needing a plan. Like the franchisee that has a set program to follow, certain real estate investors know exactly what they need to do to maximize a property's value. And yet, as we'll learn later on, a business plan is useful in many such situations. Similarly, existing businesses may be surprised by where a plan may lead...

Pat

Pat was the proud owner of a successful plumbing business. He had put the last several years into growing the business. It was now positioned to go to the next level and seek out large government and public works projects. Pat knew writing business plans wasn't one of his key strengths. He liked the idea of an independent advisor bringing new thoughts and ideas to his business. So Pat hired a consulting firm to help him "invent the future" and they worked together closely to create a six-year plan for his business.

The plan and the process of creating it were eye openers for Pat. Through the process suggestions were made on how to streamline inventory controls and save money using vendor discounts for prompt payment. While this was basic information it was never taught in school and his friendly competitors, naturally, never revealed such strategies. The biggest weakness and opportunity uncovered was that Pat's company needed to increase their bonding limit so that it could pursue higher dollar projects. Although each state was different, Pat knew that his state's contractor's licensing division required a bond be posted for a maximum dollar amount of work to be done. So, for example, a $100,000 bond allowed Pat's company to bid jobs up to $1 million. The bond was issued by a surety or bank or insurance company and cost Pat $10,000, or 10% of the $100,000 face value per year. The plan suggested the bonding limit be increased to $1 million. Pat was in a growing area and large public works projects were headed his way. The plan suggested that a higher bonding would allow Pat to partake in such projects.

The plan contained great information for Pat. He immediately went to his bank to see how the increased bonding could be financed. This banker indicated they would consider Pat's request if he had a business plan that outlined exactly how the increased bonding would be utilized to generate greater cash flow for his company. Pat was quite pleased to hand his banker just such a document. Pat's banker was impressed. The bonding was increased shortly thereafter and Pat's company moved up to the next level of business.

Pat's case serves to illustrate the business plan benefits for existing business owners looking to expand to a new level. Whether you are a new company or have been around for 200 years, it is never too late in the business cycle to obtain and utilize fresh ideas and new approaches.

There are many strategic reasons for why a business plan makes sense. You might want a plan to take to potential investors and/or lenders in order to expand or rejuvenate your business. Or maybe you sense flaws in your organization -- you're not sure of your long-term goals, pricing is based on your mood, management styles change with every personnel change and the like. Small problems and even smaller poor choices can add up fast. Don't wait for all the little problems to begin spiraling into a vortex that can take your business straight down the tubes.

Using your Plan

First, you need a business plan to get to know your business and to create the path that will describe how you will get from where you are to where you want to be. Sure, you might be able to find success without a plan. You might be able to get from Pismo Beach to Cape Hatteras without a map, but wouldn't it be easier with one?

In addition to helping you create appropriate strategies for your business, a winning plan can help sell your ideas to customers (especially if you are pursuing a business that goes after large contracts) and employees as well. Think creatively and use your plan as a serious marketing tool.

A truly effective business plan should build ownership in key players. Don't just write the plan on your own and stick it in a drawer. Involve significant others (partners, managers, family) wherever and whenever you can because many of them will play key roles in making your dream a reality. Keep employees and partners involved in the planning, preparation and use of your business plan. Encourage those who will be most impacted by the plan to take an interest in the continuing and evolving life of the plan.

Investors and lenders aren't out there giving away money with no thought. (If they are, please call me!) Potential funders (loan committees, family, friends, venture capitalists, stockholders) will need to evaluate your business in order to make a decision as to whether or not your business is a safe risk. Your business plan is the document that gives them information they need in order to accurately make an evaluation. It is your chance to sell others on your business idea and strategy. Use your plan to get investors and lenders on board and then continue to use it to lead your business.

It should be noted that when you use your business plan to raise money all the federal and state securities laws must be followed. Typically, a private placement memorandum (or "PPM") is prepared by a securities attorney. The PPM contains all the risks an investor must be aware of and a subscription agreement for shares whereby the investor indicates he is aware of all the risks. The business plan is incorporated into the PPM so the investor has an understanding of where the company is headed. While a complete discussion of the securities laws is beyond the scope of this book and we recommend that you seek qualified legal counsel and financial advice. We shall also review this issue again in Chapter 10.

Keep in mind that different potential funding entities have different interests when it comes to business investment and they will be making an immediate initial decision as to whether or not you capture their interest. You have maybe ten minutes to get a funder's interest and instill in him or her a sense of confidence in your ability to pay back or increase his or her investment. Most entities will be looking for an interesting idea, virtually guaranteed cash flow and the business acumen to bring it all together.

Your first chance to wow your audience is with your executive summary. It's your first impression, so it has to be powerful. It has to be captivating and promising. It lets the reader know that you have a well thought out, winning idea for a business, product, service and/or market niche and the team and systems capabilities to fully capitalize on it. If the executive summary does not deliver, the rest of the plan will not be read.

After the executive summary, potential funders may look to the numbers to see if your ideas can generate the kind of revenues they are looking for. Potential investors and lenders often look first to your income projections and then to the balance sheet and income statement to see if those projections are realistic. Non-equity funders (the kind that are not looking to share in a piece of the business) will look to your forecasts to see if and how you will be able to repay loans. Equity funders (the kind that want some ownership in your business) will also be looking for evidence of a market. But don't think you can simply state that there is a market for your business. Don't bother. The reader will analyze the work you present and make a determination on their own.

If the executive summary shows an interesting idea and the financials show a possibility of financial return, then the next (and perhaps last) section the potential lender or investor may turn to will be a quick review of your background and that of other pertinent management personnel. All the great plans in the world will be worthless in the hands of incompetent or less than ethical owners and/or managers. Potential lenders and investors will be looking for experience, education and evidence that you can handle all you have promised.

Rich Dad Tips

- The executive summary is your calling card. The way it is written will immediately tell a savvy investor or lender if you have the experience and expertise to lead a business. If it isn't a winner, the plan may never be read.

- When you initially begin sending out your business plan to investors or lenders, send it to a small portion of your potential universe so that you can get feedback. If you are off the mark, you'd rather know early and adjust. Make sure to ask for open and honest feedback (and be ready to hear it) from the people who tell you "no." They will offer valuable advice.

- Remember again that Money follows great management. Many good business plans don't attract money not because the deal did not attract cash but because the person controlling the deal did not attract the cash. The key to success is people, people and people. Emphasize you and your team's track record in the executive summary.

- Keep the plan clear and concise. If complicated and technical writings must be included, place them at the end with supporting documents.

The preparation of your plan will help you figure out how much funding you need. But don't skip it if you are fortunate enough to need no outside funding at all. Preparation of your plan will help you plan your income and expenses, your profits and losses, and thus show you whether or not a particular business can realistically be expected to meet your financial goals.

Whether you are preparing your plan to strategize your business or to get funding (or for both reasons), don't get so caught up in one aspect that you neglect the other. Balance is key. So is remembering that every section of your plan will likely be of primary importance to someone.

What are some of the hassles you might be saved from if you take the time to prepare a business plan? How about quitting your day job only to find your great idea won't pay the mortgage? Or resorting to high interest credit cards to finance the business? Many businesses fail within the first five years. Of those that fail, a staggeringly high percentage of them do not have business plans. Of course, the credit card companies don't care if you fail, with our without a business plan. They want their money. So before you risk it all plan ahead, but be prepared for the unexpected and don't be afraid to make mistakes.

Gathering Materials

The materials you choose to include in your plan will depend on the specifics of your business and whether or not you are using the plan to secure funding. Most plans that will be used to get funding will include a capital equipment and supply list, balance sheet, break-even analysis, income projection statements, cash flow statements and a loan application.

You should also include an explanation as to the assumptions used for projections. Other materials might include: organizational charts, management bios and/or resumes, market data and a list of who is going to receive the document. And, as mentioned, in many cases the securities laws will have to be followed as well.

The last section of your plan will be Support Materials. Though support materials compose the back end of the business plan, don't wait until the end to start gathering them. As you write the text of your plan, you will hopefully realize what documents and information you will want to attach. Get a notebook and keep a running list as you write. Take time as you finish each section to determine if you have the support documents listed. If you do not have them, make the appropriate calls to get them. Some documents may take awhile to get to you. By making the requests as you go, rather than waiting to do it all at the end, you will save yourself a lot of time. As you will find, gathering materials almost takes as much time as the more important thought process behind the plan. The actual writing should go smoothly and quickly if you are well organized and have done enough homework to know how turn your idea into a winning business.

As you are going through the time-consuming process of gathering materials and conducting research, keep your eyes and ears open for news that is even remotely related to your business idea. Clip newspaper articles, check out books, request transcripts of radio shows. Anything that deals with your business, your market, your industry or the overall economy and regulatory environment can be useful. Consider it just another aspect of research that accompanies your personal learning from advisors, peers and mentors. It is critical that you learn the brutal "street smart" realities of your business.

Start a file system for all the information you will be gathering. You might consider breaking up information into pertinent subject headings that reflect the subject headings of your plan. Or you might want to break out information by date or source – whatever works for you. As you come across new leads or new information, stick it in the appropriate file. Then when you get down to the business of preparing each individual section, you will have at least some of your research already done.

The Issue With Questions Posed

You will note as we go through this book that a lot of questions get asked. For example, in the chapter of Marketing, many questions are asked on the nature and the type of your customers. These questions aren't posed to harass or burden you. Instead, they are important considerations for you to review. They are put forth to get you thinking about what to write about. Like a snowflake, every business plan is unique and different. No two are alike. Different questions must be addressed and answered in each plan. But like a flake, if you totally ignore all of the questions you won't have much to show for your efforts.

So when you are reading a list of questions to be addressed, pick out the ones that pertain to your business. And then answer them in your plan. Don't let your eyes glaze over as you read the questions. Instead, keep them to pick out the ones that will allow you to prepare a winning business plan.

Chapter Four

Mission and Goals

"If you don't know where you are going, every road will get you nowhere."
– Henry Kissinger

Why are you in business?

Sophisticated investors and lenders want a peek into your heart to see if you have what it takes to be successful. Their answer often lies in your mission statement. A company's mission is sacred to true entrepreneurs because it is the essence of who they are and why they are in business. In Rich Dad's B-I Triangle the mission is the foundation and bedrock of a company. Not having a strong and clear mission is unacceptable because it answers the most important question of all, "Why are you in business?" If your motivation isn't strong enough, nothing else matters.

All for-profit businesses are in business to make money, hence the name for-profit. The question is:

1) Are you in business first to serve people and second to make money? or
2) Are you in business to first make money and second serve people?

Many novices fail to recognize that a business which seeks money over a higher purpose has no soul. The answer to the above question is that great entrepreneurs are in business to both make money and serve a higher purpose. They key is balance. When one motivation becomes too great it begins to harm a business.

Great entrepreneurs balance their business mission with their spiritual mission because both are essential and linked to one another. Rarely will a business without a strong sense of purpose survive, especially during the beginning stages because it is a team's desire to genuinely make a difference that inspires it to weather the trials every business goes through.

A company's mission also helps it maintain focus throughout its life. As a compass for the company, it provides a strong sense of direction to you as a reminder of why you got into business and what direction you ought to head. The mission provides a useful benchmark to evaluate opportunities and set goals.

It is often helpful to explore your intentions on paper. Putting pen to paper helps put your thoughts in order, helps you see connections you aren't making in your head. Try getting a journal and a good pen and write about your intentions, your wants, dreams and needs. Don't think, just write. Start a page with a question and just keep going until you fill a few pages. Try this exercise for a week or two and then go back and read through what you have written with an eye toward patterns. Look for repetitive words and themes.

Here are a few ideas to get you started:

"I have always wanted to..."
"If I knew I could not fail, I would..."
"I will be good at my business because..."
"I want to offer my product or service because..."
"In five years, my business will..."
"I am best at...?"
"I can make the biggest difference in the world by...
"I can serve the most people by..."

Goal Setting

If you think of your mission as a compass, you can consider your goals the map. Goals are the step-by-step plans that will make your dreams come true.

It's a lot easier to get what you want if you know what you want. Though your personal goals may not be spelled out explicitly in your business plan, they will color all aspects of your plan and thus your business. What are your personal and business goals? Are you in it for the freedom? Do you want financial security in the long haul? If so, what does that security look like? What is your exit strategy? Do you want to eventually go public? Do you want to establish a business that can be sold for a large profit? Do you want to have a thriving business legacy to leave to your children? What about franchising or establishing multiple locations? (See, we just threw a lot of questions your way. You may not want to answer every one of them. But answering at least one of these questions is important for you. Good. Now, back to our narrative.)

Odds are you didn't decide to start a business because you like the long hours and personal/family sacrifice that go along with such a venture. Instead, the odds are that you see payoffs for your time and effort and the ability to make a difference to society. Those payoffs are a good place to start your review of mission and goals. What do you want out of your business?

Your main goals should be measurable in time, dollars, quantity or comparison. You might have goals of a certain amount of profit (dollars) for a certain number of items (quantity) by a certain date (time). Your goals might include a particular ranking in the market (comparison) or a percentage improvement (comparison) or a number of days without injury (time and comparison). If you can't measure it, it's not a goal. For example, wanting to be the best in the business is not a good goal unless you can measure "the best" in dollars, quantity, or other concrete comparison.

You will also have steps you can take to achieve your goals. These steps can be considered support goals or tactics. Support goals are more strategic than primary goals. For example, if your goal is to decrease injuries by 20 percent, your support goals might include holding a worker safety seminar, implementing a worker safety plan or establishing fines for unsafe conditions (or rewards for safe performance).

Remember that the business plan is only an overall guide, not a step-by-step accounting of business practices. This is not only due to a need for brevity, but also due to the fact that business plans often make it into public hands (especially in the case of a public offering). Don't put anything in your plan that you wouldn't want to see in the newspaper. Better safe than sorry.

Whatever goals (primary or support) you decide to set for your business, be sure to write them down. Add your goals to your journal for a few weeks before you start writing your plan. Do your journaling the way it best suits you. If you get struggle with the all-consuming blank page, try writing in your journal whenever you get a new idea. Buy some brightly colored pens and choose a journal with a picture or texture that inspires you. If you are the type to just get down to business, set aside time each day to sit down with a good, sturdy journal and a reliable black pen. Whatever your style, take the necessary step of exploring your dreams and goals on paper.

When writing in your journal, be as specific as you can. Use all your senses. What will your perfect business look like? How will you feel about it? What sounds do you hear (peace and quiet, a busily ringing cash register)? Really put yourself in the place and time you are striving to reach. Think about the steps you will take. Think about the outcomes. Think about alternatives and what-ifs. Think about what life will be like five, ten or even twenty years from now.

Don't worry about the business plan when you are goal-setting or exploring your dreams. That comes later. Thinking too far ahead at this early stage can derail the process as fear turns to procrastination. For now, just let your mind fly. You will likely use some of the material you put down in a goal/objective section of your business plan (not all plans include such a section) or as part of your mission statement. Even what you never put in your plan will be useful.

So, after all this journal writing, are you ready for brevity?

Mission Statement

Can you now summarize your mission into a single sentence? That is the aim of a mission statement. To succinctly put forth the main reason why you are in business. The mission statement should briefly describe what you do and what makes you special. Investors, friends, and family will use this one sentence to form an impression of the opportunity.

Rich Dad Tips

- Most people start a business only to make money, not recognizing that money for money's sake is not a strong enough mission. Money alone does not provide enough fire, drive or desire.

- The mission of a business should fill a need that the customers want, and if it fills that need, and fills it well, the business will begin to make money. Think first to serve people and then to make money. Often the more you people serve the more successful you become.

- Listen carefully to your inner thoughts and deep dreams during the mission writing process. Great plans come from simple, clear and grand missions that inspire your heart and soul.

Chapter Five

Executive Summary and Business Strategy

*"What is conceived well is expressed clearly, and the words
to say it will arrive with ease."*
– Nicolas Boileau

Executive Summary

This is a section that must be included in your plan. It is the first and most read section of any business plan and needs to given great emphasis.

Your executive summary is a summary of your business that answers all the key questions (why, who, what, when, where, how). Though it is the first section of the plan, write it last. If you try to write your executive summary first, it will likely be the hardest thing you ever write. If you write it at the end, after you've thoroughly thought through your unique products and systems, built your team of mentors and advisors, researched your market and competition, planned your financial needs and potential earnings and analyzed your business' strengths and weaknesses, it will come much more easily.

What information does an executive summary include? The basics. Include the name and type of business (including its legal structure) and required investment or loan information (the amount and purpose of money you are requesting and your repayment plan -- principal and interest). If the plan will be going to a lender or potential investor, be as specific as you can about the money aspects of your plan, including how you will use the money.

Even a business plan has room for dreams. Don't be afraid to include a sentence or two about why you want to (or why you wanted to) start your business. After all, "why?" is one of your key questions. This is often best answered with your mission statement and a brief description of the motivation behind your mission.

Remember to keep your executive summary short, for it is sure to be read...

Maria and Paul

Maria had an excellent idea for a new business opportunity. She and a group of colleagues had advanced engineering degrees and were involved in nanotechnology research and development. Nanotechonology is the art of manipulating materials on an atomic or molecular scale to build microscopic devices. It is considered "the next big thing" by many venture capitalists. Nearly $10 billion a year was being invested into nanotech due to its promise.

Marie's group, now incorporated under the name NanoNow, Inc., had developed a patented technique whereby nanoparticles were added to an automobile's gas tank. Their unique fuel additive worked as an oxidation catalyst to help the fuel burn cleaner. Their company name NanoNow, stood for Nanotech New Oxidation Winner. Of course, everyone wanted cleaner burning fuel for less polluted air and for the better of the environment. But even more beneficial for Maria and her colleagues was that venture investors were currently quite interested in nanotech. Just like biotech and the internet in previous years, simply by mentioning nanotech doors were opening.

Maria was in charge of writing the business plan. NanoNow was seeking to raise $50 million in a first round of funding to begin commercializing their patented technology. The plan discussed the market, their competitors and their unique patented position in the industry. It was a 300 page well supported and convincing scientific argument for investing in NanoNow.

Paul was a business consultant who helped entrepreneurs shape their business plans. While he liked all the work Marie had put in on such a detailed business plan, he also knew that not only is brevity the soul of wit, it also defines the soul of many venture capitalists. They want the brevity of a hot business area times dollars invested to equal huge quick gains. Demonstrating that magic, vault-opening equation in 30 or even 300 pages was one task. But condensing the equation into a one page Executive Summary was an art.

Paul knew that the venture investors didn't have time for a long and detailed narrative. Their assistants could wade through all that. Instead, they wanted one persuasive page, which after reading, they could snap their fingers and bark, "Check it out."

This is why Paul was so focused on getting Maria and her group to write an effective Executive Summary. One page meant the difference between $50 million or continued polluted air. It was an important page. But Maria and company were engineers. They weren't used to brief persuasion. Everything had to be proven and re-proven. Maria said she couldn't possibly summarize and persuade in one page.

Paul had seen it before. Many of his clients could write a brief and winning Executive Summary in their sleep. But for engineers and other technical types it was nearly an impossible task. They just weren't trained to write that way. As a result, Paul had a previously utilized solution to the problem. He hired a copywriter to write the Executive Summary. The copywriter was used to writing short, persuasive copy. He knew which buttons to push and where in the copy to push them. He was the expert they needed.

As it turned out, with a persuasive one pager for the venture guys and voluminous material for the underlings to check out, NanoNow was funded. Maria and her colleagues went on to great technical and financial heights without ever fully appreciating how influential the art of an Executive Summary was to their success.

Again, it is important to remember that an Executive Summary should do what it says: summarize the business plan. It should be very short (one page is ideal), and should highlight the most important sections of the plan. Beware, it may be the hardest thing you write during the planning process. Condensing 30 to 40 pages (or in Maria's case many more) down to their very essence takes an intense understanding of the subject matter and considerable writing skill. It is best left until you have written all other parts of the plan and have come to a thorough understanding of all the subjects. Your plan should be well conceived before you start writing the summary.

If you are using your business plan to attract funding, you might think of the plan as a resume for your business. Your business plan sets out all the reasons why someone would want to give you money. And just as an employer has to look at dozens, sometimes hundreds of resumes in a short period of time in order to narrow down the prospects to that hopeful few who will be called back for an interview, so do potential investors need to sift through piles and piles of business plans in order to find that hopeful few who will get a closer reading and even an interview. The timeline for potential investors is similarly short. Some investment decision-makers must go through as many as one hundred plans a week. Obviously they can't do that without getting good at quickly separating the wheat from the chaff. You need to be able to summarize all the essentials in a way that will entice readers and back up that enticement with confidence. This, in a nutshell, is the job of your executive summary.

One way to compose the executive summary is to summarize each section of the plan in no more than a paragraph per section. If you find you can't do that, your plan (or particular sections) may not be sufficiently focused or you may not thoroughly understand the components you have put into the plan.

Try to make your executive summary a concise selling tool. Leave out sections that do not show the company in its best light -- such as the weakness portion of the Strengths and Weaknesses subsection. Your executive summary may be one section or you might want to break it down into briefer subsections. If tables or bullet lists will save you space without losing clarity, consider using them.

Timelines

Writing a business plan can take as little or as much time as you let it. There is no right amount of time other than exactly how long it takes you to get it done. Try to work with advisors and mentors to set goals for each section. Have them hold you accountable to get them done as an added incentive to stay on track. The reality, however, is that if you have to be held accountable by others to get the sections done you should ask if you have true entrepreneurial spirit.

If you need someone to push you along to write a plan, ask yourself who will be there to push you along when you're in the midst of a crisis. Listen closely to your inner voice while you write your plan. Indicators like how well you commit to meeting deadlines for timelines can tell you just how willing you are to do what needs to be done to creating a winning business. The determination to write a plan needs to be amplified 100 times to succeed in business. The fuel for that amplification must come directly from your passion and no one else. That is how you join the ranks of the elusive 5% of businesses that succeed.

Strategy

Your business plan is a long-term planning document and it will cover a lot of ground. In this section you will paint a picture with words that brings to life how you will get your business started and how you will continuously grow and improve it for the next three to five years. Equally important, preparing your business plan will help you figure out how you define success and what steps you will need to take in order to reach that definition.

Build a strategy for tackling the process of writing a business plan. Here are some tips for business plan preparation:

- Start with the words. The words drive the numbers.
- Beware of technical jargon. Keep the tone conversational.

- Be concise and clear. Short, crisp sentences add authority. Bullet lists are friendly.
- Work on the sections you find hardest first.
- Include mentors, advisors, family and partners in goal setting.
- Don't be afraid to hire professionals, but don't delegate decision making.
- Always be realistic (but positive) about your business.
- Be honest, especially when it comes to shortcomings and risks.
- Use a spell-checker and grammar checker. Your plan will be judged not only by the ideas it presents, but also by its presentation and accuracy. Don't let your business acumen come into question just because your grasp of language isn't what it could be.
- Only include what's relevant. Don't do your thinking in your plan; do it before.
- Remember that the final goal is not a completed business plan, nor is it the acquisition of funding. Rather, the final goal is the realization of your business goals as set out in your plan.
- Embrace the fact that your business plan will never be finished. A business is an ever-changing entity and your plan is no different.
- Keep the key words -- who, what, when, where, why, how -- at the forefront of your thoughts as well as the forefront of your text. Answer each of the key questions in the first paragraph of each section. The rest of each section will be simple expansion.
- Intimately know the basics of your business strategy before you start writing.
- Start gathering information before you need it -- market information, competition facts, etc.
- Only include relevant financial and operational details.
- Don't make grandiose promises or representations to yourself or others (especially potential investors).
- Allow more room for detail on those sections particularly relevant to your business.

- Let your specific needs and goals dictate the structure of your plan.
- Use charts wherever you can to save space if doing so does not eliminate important detail.
- Work on making your document as visually pleasing as possible.

Looking Forward

When you project the future, you will need to take into consideration where you want your business to be. Be specific but recognize you are making an educated guess. This is where a team of experienced advisors and mentors can add great credibility to your plan. Ask yourself key questions. What will your workforce look like? What will your costs and income be? What expansions and new technologies will you have introduced? What will your loan balances be? Will you have investors? Who will be your customers? What will your market share be? What will your advertising and/or marketing look like and how will it be used? What will your role be in the business?

In addition, you will need to understand the industry, your market, the political climate, economic trends and every other aspect of an intricately woven web of relationships and challenges. You can help yourself and your business by staying abreast of world, national, state and local issues.

You don't have to be a mind reader to forecast trends. Simply staying aware and doing some consistent study will put you ahead of the game.

Rich Dad Tips

- Savvy investors know that every projection in a five year business plan is a guess. History is a great indicator of the future, so make sure you benchmark similar companies to ensure the investor or lender that you have a firm grasp on industry dynamics.

- Comparing your projected financials to others in the industry in the appendix of the plan is another useful tool.

There is another large issue that arises when you provide forward looking projections. You shouldn't be overly optimistic or overly certain of success, especially when seeking to raise money. Looking into the future is necessary, but you shouldn't use a far off date to claim that certain profit levels and grand milestones will be reached. Those kind of positive representations, especially when written into your plan, become potential and problematic misrepresentations, especially when investor monies and attorneys are involved. There is no guarantee of success in any business. Forward looking statements as to profits and performance must be made cautiously and conditionally. The SEC (the Securities and Exchange Commission, the U.S. government agency which regulates the sale of stock) has an entire set of guidelines for forward-looking statements. They suggest using conditional language such as 'we believe that...' instead of 'we guarantee that...' and 'it is our opinion that...' instead of 'it is certain that...' While the less than 100% positive conditional language may sound wimpy, there are two important points to consider. First, sophisticated investors are used to reading this kind of wording. It is not going to dissuade them from investing. In fact, by failing to use conditional language they'll wonder if you really know what you are doing. After all, why wouldn't a prudent business person use the SEC's suggested language if it could help them avoid a lawsuit? Remember, it is your responsibility to seek legal advice with any claims or assertions in your business plan to protect yourself from liability issues.

Secondly, let's remember what we are doing here. We are talking about the future. There are no guarantees or certainties. By using conditioned language you are giving yourself the necessary flexibility to account for the many changes that lie ahead. Don't lock your plan, or yourself, in to a fixed view of what lies ahead. Reserve the right to get smarter in the future!

Finding Expert Advice

In a perfect world, you would have the time and expertise to prepare your business plan completely with yourself and your closest advisors. When you prepare your own plan, you are so intimately familiar with it that its use becomes a natural outgrowth of the preparation process. However, few of us have the management, organizational, writing and editing, planning, layout and design, marketing and financial expertise it takes to prepare an effective plan. And even those who might have the expertise likely don't have the time.

There are a variety of experts from whom you should solicit help in the preparation process. You might want to consider engaging the counsel of retired executives in your field, peers in non-competitive business, entrepreneur groups, your attorney, your CPA, friendly sophisticated investors or lenders, management consultants, marketing/PR experts, a business coach, a writer/editor, a graphic designer, and a printer. Some companies specialize in business plan preparation and offer all the needed expertise under one roof.

Never completely hand off the job. It is your business. It will be your plan. You are the one who will be using the plan. Meet with your experts and planners at set times throughout the process, so that you stay up-to-date. Don't go through the expense and time of having others prepare a plan that you cannot or will not use.

Want to know if you are involved enough in the planning process? A simple test is to write your own executive summary and mission statement (you may want to do this prior to the planning process, as well as at the end). Then let your planners or experts do the same and compare. This way you can be sure you not only understand your plan, but that your planners or experts understand your business as well.

Chapter Six

Know Your Business

*"Business is never so healthy as when, like a chicken, it must do a
certain amount of scratching for what it gets."*
– Henry Ford

The better you understand your business, the better prepared you are to write the business plan. Ideally, you will have thoroughly thought out your business long before you ever open your doors for sales. Too many entrepreneurs jump into business with both feet and don't bother with understanding (let alone planning) until the water is rising. Jumping into the deep end of the pool is not the best way to learn to swim. If you're lucky, you won't drown, but even if you make it out of the pool, the experience is likely to be remarkably unpleasant.

The Business Section

The first major part of your business plan should be a detailed description of your business. You'll address your corporate entity choice between a corporation or a limited liability company. Don't consider using a sole proprietorship or general partnership. Investors won't even bother reading the plan because there is too much personal liability. To fully appreciate this see my book *Start Your Own Corporation*. Your detailed description will also include strengths and weaknesses, a description of your operations, location, personnel, records, insurance and security. Once again, money follows good management. It's important to emphasize the experience, education and track record of your people.

For The Business, The Market and The Financials sections of your plan, it is best to introduce the section with a brief one-page summary. From there, you can use more detailed subsections. While the entire plan should be succinct, these summaries will allow interested parties to graze for pertinent information.

There are two questions to ask yourself about your business that color every part of this section, though their answers are never directly addressed in the plan:

Why are you in business?

What is your business?

If these seem like easy questions to you, you've either done a good job thinking through your business or you haven't even started. We'll hope for the former.

Why are you in business? How well do you know yourself, in particular, your personal motivations? When you decided to go into business, was it out of desperation (lost job, family illness, personal injury)? It's okay for desperation to spur you into a new direction, but don't let it rush you. Did you decide to go into business out of a desire for personal fulfillment (following a dream, helping others)? Many businesses are begun for one of these reasons, but if you don't understand the realities of owning and operating a business, you aren't likely to stay in business long enough to do you or anyone else any good. Did you decide to start a business in hopes of amassing great riches? This is another common reason, but chasing after dollars runs the risk of leading to early burnout and/or disillusionment. Understand your motivations and you can guard against many a typical disaster.

What is your business? Don't answer too quickly. Just because you sell office supplies does not necessarily mean you want to look and feel like all the competitors. Think about it: there are plenty of office supply stores out there. Most are better established than yours. Many will have lower prices than yours. So why should anyone go to your store? Answer that question and you will know what business you are really in. Do you offer faster service and delivery? Do you have a specialized staff that can help clients with organization, technology or planning? What is it that your customers (or potential customers) say about your business when recommending it to friends? What part of the idea for your business originally got you so excited that you couldn't wait to tell your family about it? When it comes to identifying the heart of your business, look to your own heart. Concentrate on what your business is rather than what it does. Think back to the spiritual mission and business mission section and ponder what higher purpose you have to serve that will differentiate you in your space and allow you to generate cash flow.

With the answers to these two deceptively simple questions, you will hopefully find the key that unlocks the potential of your business idea -- an identity that can't be duplicated. And it is that identity that will garner you funding, investors and customers. But first we've got to overcome one of the toughest parts of business plan authorship -- writing about your strengths and weaknesses.

Mikhail

Mikhail was stuck. He needed to finish his business plan in the next two days for a potential investor but couldn't get past the next section on his template: Strengths and Weaknesses.

Strengths and Weaknesses. How could he write about that?

"Our company's strength is me. I'm the best taco maker on earth."

He couldn't write that, even if it was true. It seemed too brazen, like a tedious NFL show-off player dancing wildly in the end zone. That wasn't Mikhail's style.

And weaknesses? How was he supposed to handle that one?

"Our company's weakness is that management has no idea how to write a business plan."

Again, while true, it didn't inspire much confidence.

Acknowledging his writer's block, Mikhail left the house and walked down to Starbucks for a toffee latte something. Standing in line he ran into

Jill, a new friend who had done well starting and selling several businesses. He told her of his barrier to completing the plan. She offered to help and they sat down to brainstorm with their vessels of caffeine and sugar.

Jill agreed that in the business plans she had worked on before, the strengths and weakness section had always been hard to write. But she noted it was a positive part of the process because it forced you to think about some crucial issues.

Why would someone really want to invest in you?

Just what *are* your strengths and weaknesses?

Are your strengths common or competitive?

Can your weaknesses be overcome?

While talking about Mikhail's business, and after several latte refuelings, some headway was achieved. Mikhail did indeed make an excellent taco. He infused them with all sorts of unique combinations, from mangoes to margarita-marinated mahi mahi. His strengths were both common -- he was good at making tacos -- and competitive -- he made them better than anyone else around. Jill suggested he focus on these issues as his strengths. Mikhail didn't have to be brazen to make such claims, she said. A section beginning with: "Management believes that its strengths are found in its ability to prepare unique and flavorful tacos" would work.

The weakness section she said was the trickier one. Just as strengths came in two varieties, common and competitive, so did weaknesses. They were either common or catastrophic.

After reviewing his plans some more Jill didn't see anything that would stand out as an obvious catastrophic weakness. Was there a risk that the entire country would turn away from Mexican food? Not likely. Was there a risk of mad taco disease? Again, not likely.

But Jill did see a common weakness and, she said with a smile, it was in this section where you turned a negative into a positive.

Mikhail made a great taco. The weakness, which was common to many new businesses, was that no one knew this. The company was weak for brand awareness. This, of course, could be overcome.

The other obvious weakness was that Mikhail was a recent Russian immigrant. Who would ever expect a former Moscow bicycle mechanic to be creative genius when it came to Mexican cuisine?

Jill saw this possible weakness as a huge potential strength. The human interest angle alone-Russian immigrant/Mexican cuisine only in America-would help turn a lack of brand awareness into a branding strength.

Mikhail was on his fourth latte and saw her vision clearly. He wanted to get back home and start writing. Jill laughed and said she understood. She also asked to see the business plan when it was finished. She knew some people who may be interested.

Before we further discuss the Strengths and Weaknesses section, it is important to underscore a key element of the story. Business plans aren't always (or best) written in a vacuum. When you are blocked or struggling with a section, clear your head and seek out the perspective, insight or just different view of someone you trust. It is amazing what human interaction can do for breaking through a tough section. And, with the benefit of additional input and review, you will find yourself drafting a better plan.

Part of gaining an intimate knowledge of your business is understanding your strengths and weaknesses (also called Core Competencies and Potential Liabilities or Competitive Advantages and Competitive Challenges and often given its own section). Think back to everything you've ever learned about competition and marketing (or skip ahead and read Chapter 8 on Marketing). At their most basic, competition and marketing are about exploiting the weaknesses of other businesses and/ or playing to the strengths of your own business. Analyze your business and think like a competitor. What strengths would a competitor try to downplay or neutralize? What weaknesses would a competitor want to highlight?

Once you have identified strengths and weaknesses you can begin to plan accordingly. Are there strengths that are currently underutilized? What might you do to take advantage of your unique attributes? Are there weak points that you can shore up -- through training, strategic hiring, team building, organization or planning? What can you do now to limit the marketing options of your competitors later? Focusing on strengths and weaknesses will lead to better decisions as you proceed.

Strengths

As discussed in the story, there are two basic categories of strengths a business can exhibit: common and competitive. A common strength is something you do well. A competitive strength is something you do better than others in your field.

How a company exhibits strength -- through corporate vision, product, operations, marketing or sales -- may change from business to business, but will inevitably fall into one of the two categories. Knowing if your strengths are common or competitive can be difficult to determine. But it can be extremely useful when understood. A business can improve through common strengths. A business can dominate through competitive strengths.

What are your strengths? It shouldn't be a tough one to answer if you have a compelling business strategy. Challenge your idea's reason for being if it doesn't have clear strengths.

Consider that business strengths are noticed by two groups: competitors and customers. What they see will help you understand what you've got. Customers (hopefully) will notice product strengths (lower price, higher quality, better variety) in individual products or through positive brand associations. A strong brand can encompass a number of individual products and enhance the perceived positives of all. For example, the Coca-Cola brand extends to and benefits Sprite, Diet Coke and even Mr. Pibb.

Operational strengths such as logistics may not be overtly noticed by customers, but they will feel the effects of such strengths. Higher efficiency will mean lower prices, faster service and fewer mistakes. Even if customers don't know why your product or service is better, they will certainly notice the end result. So will competitors and soon your strength may become a common business practice for an entire industry. But the point is that if both customers and competitors are noticing these things, whether directly or indirectly, you should notice them too and practically speaking they should be deliberate strategies in your business plan.

Sales and distribution strengths will likely not be noticed by customers. They won't care how many stores carry your product or how good your contracts are. All they know is whether or not they want to buy your product or service at any particular point in time. But they can't buy if they are not exposed to your product or service. Distribution controls that exposure. Sales come from an ability to turn exposure into commitment. As such, sales and distribution strengths are key, and an area your competitors will be sizing you up on. If they are noticing your strength, so should you.

Unique leadership skills or corporate vision can create highly advantageous employee and vendor loyalty. It can also increase sales through good distribution relationships. There can be huge benefits from such skill and vision. That said, none of it may be noticed outside the corporate structure. Until, that is, your competitors wonder why you are kicking butt while they are sitting still. Then corporate vision and leadership will be noticed by everyone with whom you do business -- from the mailman to the sales force to the customer. Do you notice it internally now? Have you developed it into a core competency that can be considered one of your strengths? It should all flow from your mission statement as a reflection of an organization's leader. Think back to Rich Dad's B-I Triangle, which outlines the mission, leadership and teamwork as the three pillars of a successful business.

There are many more examples to consider. Maybe you are charismatic or have a gift for motivating others. Maybe your honesty engenders loyalty in those with whom you partner. Maybe you were an accountant in a past life and have a true talent for budgeting on a shoestring. Your personal strengths may translate quite well to your business. Don't overlook your key strengths. In business, you need every one you can get.

Think widely about your strengths. Think about what you do well. Think about the strengths of your partners or team members. Think about what works well in your current business, if you have one. If you aren't currently in business, you will need to think creatively to highlight strengths that will realistically apply to your business. Be real and don't fool yourself. Talk to people you trust about what they think your strengths are. Do any of these strengths really help your business? Do they lead to lowering costs or increasing sales? These are the types of strengths to include in your business plan.

Know your competition. Read their business plans if you can. And keep in mind they may be reading yours. A business plan is no place for details that threaten your competitive advantage. Check out your competitor's advertising. Know their operations as intimately as you possibly can and see if they share your strengths. If they do, your strength is common. If they don't, your strengths may be competitive, and that's good for you!

Once you know your strengths, you will need to understand the whys and hows of those same strengths. Why is it a strength that you have developed a new way to track your office supply store inventory? Is it because it makes it possible to fill orders more quickly than your competition? Or is it because your system is so user-friendly for vendors that they give you a break on your contracts? Or maybe your tracking has opened up an entirely new route for getting your product exposed to customers.

How did your skill, service, product or idea become a strength? Was it through innovative use? Was advertising a key? Did you discover it on your own through research or study? Or did you learn it from watching how another company does things? How did your customers become aware of the benefit of your strength to them? By understanding the hows and whys, you increase your chances of repeating your strengths in other areas while playing them up throughout the company and through customer awareness. The bottom line is: strengths are strengths because they serve customers which results in strengthened profits.

Rich Dad Tips

- If you don't possess the right skills or strengths for a business, communicate how you surrounded yourself with the right employees or advisors. You don't have to be a great mechanic to own a thriving automotive repair business. If you have great leadership and marketing skills you can hire great mechanics.

- Public company 10-K annual reports are a great source of reference material for entrepreneurial business plans. They provide benchmark costs and strategies as well as relevant industry information. Securities laws require them to disclose information that is very helpful to entrepreneurs.

Weaknesses

Examining real or potential weaknesses is not nearly as much fun as examining strengths, but it is just as important. (Don't you hate how that usually works?) And you sure don't want to write down all your weaknesses, print them on good paper and then hand them to other people to read.

The problem is that while this may not be a section you want to shout from the rooftop to potential investors or lenders, it is one of the most useful sections for you as an entrepreneur. Our greatest weaknesses are our blind spots, which we rarely see in ourselves. Most great entrepreneurs surround themselves with people who tell them the good, the bad and the ugly because confronting the brutal facts is the best way to achieve progress on those elements of the business that are holding you back. Novice entrepreneurs hide issues and great entrepreneurs seek to identify issues.

Just as with strengths, weaknesses fall into two general categories: common and catastrophic. Common weaknesses are those that you share with a lot of other businesses such as startup hurdles, learning curves and cash flow. As long as you are generally as good as the industry standard, you'll likely be okay, although you may not excel. Catastrophic weaknesses are those that consistently put you at the bottom of the pile. Another way to look at it is that common weaknesses are those that can or will be overcome. You will eventually learn how to use your inventory software or hire someone to take over those duties, you will eventually work out an efficient order fulfillment system, and/or you will eventually have enough money to kick off that dream ad campaign. Catastrophic weaknesses are those that you can't or won't overcome. These may include a fatal error in a software program that can't be remedied, the use of someone else's intellectual property, coming in second in the race to introduce new technology and the worst weakness of all, arrogance.

Obviously, doing the footwork for your business plan should help you eliminate many of your common weaknesses before you begin your business or before you continue to the next phase of business. But the identification of catastrophic weaknesses should make you rethink your entire plan. Do you really want to put all of your time and energy into something that has a very high likelihood of failure? Aren't there other businesses to pursue that have a greater likelihood of success? Some of the best business plans are the ones you throw in the garbage because you learned from them and moved on to a better idea. Fatal flaws usually don't get better.

Just as with strengths, weaknesses can be perceived by customers and/or competitors. Your weakness could be in poor product quality, noncompetitive pricing or a lack of variety. Distribution may be your weakness if you can't keep your products on the shelves or on enough shelves to have an impact.

Operational weaknesses are frequent killers of great ideas. Many a creative person has thought up a fabulous idea only to be thwarted by the business realties of deadlines, inventory, budgets, cash flow, customer service, distribution and management. Knowing your weaknesses in these areas going in will help you pick partners and personnel to fill in the gaps. Don't be afraid to admit you might not know everything. You can always build a team that does. Never has Robert Kiyosaki's RichDad's quote

"Business and investing are team sports" been more applicable than when it comes to putting together a business team and business plan.

When focusing on weaknesses, consider that perhaps your weakness isn't so much *your* weakness as much as a competitor's strength. If you are in an industry ruled by one or two brands, it will be hard to break in and then break out with your own brand identity. Advertising is key for brand identity. In order to build your unique identity, advertising needs to be effective and visible. There is a crucial interplay between vision and volume that will ultimately determine the effectiveness of an ad campaign.

Figuring out your weaknesses (or potential weaknesses if you have not yet begun your business) is done pretty much the same way you determined your strengths. Talk to people you trust. Ask these honest and trustworthy people what they think you could improve in your company, your knowledge base and your interpersonal style. It will be hard to get an honest answer. People who like you may not want to tell you how irritating it is, for example, that you always wait four days to return a call. Emphasize to these people that you need to know now, before you quit your day job and sink your life's savings into this idea. Or be honest in explaining that your current business is hitting hard times and that sugarcoating could mean its demise. Never be afraid to guilt people into telling you the truth. It is that important. Of course, when you get the truth, take it gracefully. Say thanks so that the people who are honest with you might offer that same frankness in the future. If you pout and sulk and say they were really never your friends anyway because they implied that your lack of punctuality might be a business weakness, you are shooting your business (and yourself) in the proverbial foot. Getting honest feedback may not be pretty or fun, but if it leads to business success it is certainly worth it.

Be creative in your thinking. Try to look at every single aspect of your business. Try to imagine your product going from inspiration to sale, step by step, through all the parts of your company, from R&D to construction to employee benefits to management to advertising to sales, all with an eye toward improvement. If you were the competition and had this kind of inside information, how would you use it? If you were an average consumer, what would you want to see done differently? If you were not the business owner, but only thinking of buying the business, what would you want to see changed before you signed on the dotted line? If you were the ad agency hired to promote the business, what aspects of the company would you downplay or ignore? If you were an employee, how would you rate the business?

Create your business on paper. List everything your business will need to do (or already does). From hiring personnel to maintaining equipment, from creating a filing system to choosing a system to track your stock -- put it all down on one side of the page. Next put some thought into which areas are weak and assign a number or letter or stars or whatever suits your fancy to signify if the weakness is small, medium or great. Then write out what it would take to conquer each weakness. Finally, do a simple cost-benefit analysis and decide which of your weaknesses are worth (in time or money) eliminating. Some weaknesses you can live with, some you can't. The bottom line is: Look for weaknesses that lead to lowered sales or increased costs -- profit-eaters.

Once you have a good handle on where your weaknesses lie, fix what you can, decide which weaknesses are truly important to your businesses and put them in your plan. Choosing which weaknesses to include in your plan may be the hardest part of the preparation process. You don't want to include so many that your business looks like a failure before it even begins, but you don't want to have so few as to come off looking like a naive dreamer.

Every business has weaknesses. Seasoned professionals (the kinds who you will be asking for money from) will be able to look through your business plan and see the holes. If you want to come off as a professional as well -- as the kind of person who can take an idea and turn it into a successful business -- you need to prove you share that ability to analyze your business needs.

By pointing out what others would find on their own, you prove your abilities. But, more importantly, putting weaknesses in the plan allows you to show how you plan to eliminate or work around them. You can list a weakness and follow it with a discussion of your plans for improvement, thus showing your problem-solving skills as well as your ability to plan for the future.

Rich Dad Tips

- One weakness many new entrepreneurs have is a lack of business ownership experience or track record of results. This can be overcome by creating an advisory board of seasoned entrepreneurs who are committed to guiding you through the inevitable ups and downs of a startup business.

Chapter Seven

Know Your Real Estate

*"We can't cross a bridge until we come to it, but I always like
to lay down a pontoon ahead of time."*
– Bernard M. Baruch

James

James was a real estate investor who was ready to expand his focus.
Previously he had purchased and sold (most always for a great profit)
commercial buildings and apartment buildings.

The real estate market, as James appreciated, was always changing.
The next opportunity James wanted to pursue in his local market was
the conversion of apartments into condominium units. The combination
of young singles who wanted to buy their first property but were priced
out of the full first home market, along with the clear demographic trend
of baby boomers retiring and downsizing their living space, made for an
attractive condo market in James' city.

James had identified an upscale 400-unit apartment community as a
perfect candidate for conversion. The community had the right mix of one,
two and three-bedroom units along with the all the amenities including a
pool, community room and an excellent location.

James realized that if he could raise $4 million to acquire, convert and market the units as condominium homes, he could return a profit of between $8 million to $10 million to any investors.

When James mentioned his plan to a few friends they were immediately interested, especially when James noted that a $100,000 investment could return approximately $200,000. His friends wanted to see his plan. They wanted to know how the property would be held and why. They wanted to know how long it would take to sell all of the units. What was in the plan?

To each request James silently asked himself: "Plan? What plan?" James had never brought in partners. He had done twenty-seven real estate deals on his own. He had never needed a plan or a structure for his own individual deals before. And now, on his 28th deal, everyone wanted to see a 'plan'. And half again as many wanted to know about entities and structures for the deal as well as other issues James was not conversant in.

After the tenth request for a plan, and James' tenth response that he was working on it, he decided to begin writing the plan. Because he had never written a plan before he began researching plans by reading books and studying articles on the internet. He realize the importance of surrounding himself with great people so he created a team of advisors and also sought the help of a business plan consultant to coach him through the process.

The first consultant told James he prepared business plans for business ventures but not for real estate deals. He wasn't sure how a real estate plan was prepared and didn't know to whom he should refer James. James made five more calls and received the same deer-in-the-headlights response: "Huh?"

Finally, on the seventh call, James spoke with Ron, an experienced consultant who appreciated that a plan for a real estate venture was just as important and necessary as a business plan. Ron had prepared numerous such plans for real estate investors and developers. Ron also knew that entity structuring was an important issue for real estate investors.

Ron explained that most of the same categories for a business plan were found in a real estate plan. James explained that a number of friends were asking for 'the plan' on this deal. Ron told him not to worry. If James had no experience preparing one and needed it right away, he could use Ron or someone like him a coach to counsel him through the process. The consultant, along with Ron's group of advisors (his attorney, his CPA and his mentor) could advise him on the best legal structure to use for this project. Without going into great detail, it would most likely be a limited liability company ("LLC") or a limited partnership ("LP"): two entities that offered asset protection and flow-through taxation.

James was comfortable with Ron and hired him after checking with references and seeing samples of other plans he had participated in. The cost of hiring the right advisors to create a plan that would net him over one million was a fair price to pay.

Preparing a plan for your real estate investment can be a valuable activity. In James' case, it was the necessary vehicle for attracting investors. For other real estate activities, just as with businesses, a plan can help you think about, get to know and strategically plan for the property.

Again, just as with any business, the better you know your real estate, the better prepared you are to write your real estate plan. And in writing out your real estate plan you will identify areas for improvement and the strategies for increasing the value of property.

If you are purchasing or getting involved with your first property, it is important to ask the questions that are never directly addressed in the plan:

Why am I getting into real estate?

Can I handle all of the challenges of real estate?

The initial questions may be very easy to answer for some of you. But for those who wrestle to come up with answers, continue wrestling. It is a very useful process. Real estate is an excellent investment and retirement strategy for millions of people worldwide. But for some individuals, it can be a disaster.

So when we talk about 'know your real estate,' we are strongly suggesting that when starting out you know your tolerance for real estate.

So go for the gold. Make all the money in real estate you want. But be sure and answer the second question we have posed:

Can I handle all of the challenges of real estate?

Don't dismiss the question too quickly. If you are bringing investors into your real estate plan, they will want to see that you have experience in acquiring and managing real estate. They will want to know that you are up for the challenge.

On your first individual deal you will especially want to analyze whether you are up for the challenges. Can you handle, both financially and emotionally, tenants who don't pay and refuse to leave? Can you deal with all of the repairs that may be needed? Will you do them yourself or hire outside contractors? Will you keep enough of an eye on the property to make certain that the outside contractors don't rip you off?

Strategic and competitive advantages are somewhat less important in real estate than they are in business, but you still need to know your market and the challenges it presents. Are rents going up or down? Where are vacancy rates headed? Is the market growing or not? Talk to local brokers who are candid, honest and know the market. Such people do exist.

Insurance, record keeping and tax reporting are all lesser known but important components of successful real estate. Are you up for the challenge of essentially running a business that invests in real estate? Will you get the right insurance coverage? Will you make sure the books are kept, the bank accounts are balanced and the taxes are paid? If you can't do it, or don't have the time to do it, will you make sure it gets done?

A business plan for your real estate forces you to consider these issues. Therefore, it is a productive activity. Whether it is your first deal or your 28th like James, you need to analyze why you are getting into this particular real estate deal and whether you are up for the challenges of managing real estate, either on your own or with other partners who must be kept informed.

Accordingly, in James' case (or in your own case) consider whether you are prepared to deal with partners. Owning real estate on your own is a comparative breeze. When you add investors into the mix, there are suddenly securities law issues to be dealt with. Likewise you must deal with appropriate investor communications. The best way to look at this issue is to put yourself in your investors shoes. What type of reports and financials would you like to receive? Is yearly enough? Many state laws require a LLC or LP to hold at least annual meetings. But that is a corporate matter. In terms of financials, would annual reports satisfy you as an investor? Probably not. Like most investors, you will want to see at least quarterly financial statements. If so, you will include the representation in your business plan that financial statements will be delivered to investors every three months. And you will stick to that promise by preparing and sending out quarterly financials. Nothing gets an investor more suspicious and on edge than a failure of timely accounting.

The point of this chapter is to know your real estate and to use your business plan to know it even better. And (whether for real estate or business) when you are using a plan to attract investors, put yourself in the investor's space and think about what they want to see and hear. Draft the plan to address their concerns. And in doing so, when a promise in the plan is made, be certain to stick to it for the life of the investment.

Rich Dad Tips

- Know that large, successful real estate deals always include a business plan for each property investment. Why not take the time for each real estate deal you do?

- Consider investing a sum that is right for you in a new business so that you can review a variety of business plans from the perspective of someone who is going to put "skin in the game." It provides great perspective to walk in the shoes of your target audience.

Chapter Eight

Structure and Strategy

"Experience is the hardest kind of teacher. It gives you the test first and the lesson afterwards."
– Anonymous

Oscar

Oscar was an excellent handyman. Ever since his earliest days he could fix or repair anything. Since graduating from high school he had a truck, some tools and a loyal following. Recently, the county commission for Jerico County decided that wood-burning fireplaces had sent enough soot and smoke into the air. From now on only high efficiency gas fireplaces were allowed. While some residents complained about a loss of rights and traditions, others realized that the county was growing and if everyone kept burning wood the air would only worsen.

The new legislation was a boom for Oscar. He had a knack for installing new and approved fireplace inserts. Before long he was being actively sought after by many residents who liked the soothing nature of a fireplace. For them it didn't matter if it was wood or gas, they just wanted a flame. And word had it that Oscar was the best in Jerico County at performing the switch over.

It wasn't long before Oscar had three trucks, five employees and more business than he knew what to do with. Soon he acquired the exclusive distribution rights for a high-end fireplace manufacturer. While he was at it he started selling expensive backyard barbeque systems. In no time Oscar's business was known as Jerico Home and Hearth, the County's Fireplace and Barbeque Headquarters.

Oscar now had a showroom, even more employees and cash flow problems. He also wanted to put a second store in the growing east county area. He knew the opportunity was there but he couldn't do it all without more money.

Oscar went to Tim, his banker, to see if more money was available. Tim was a friend from high school who was very pleased with Oscar's success. But he was also concerned by Oscar's sudden growth and cash flow problems. Tim had seen first hand that growth too soon and too fast could cause severe, and even fatal, problems. The bank was not willing to increase the credit line.

Oscar took the rejection well enough. He knew he had to get a handle on his cash flow. But the opportunity for a second store was too good to be missed. If he didn't take it, someone else would. Were there any alternatives?

Tim suggested that Oscar could bring in a partner. Someone with money and perhaps some cash management experience would be a good candidate. By having the right team member on board to help out with money and advice, Oscar might be able to increase his profits even though his ownership interest was reduced.

Oscar asked how a partner was brought aboard. Tim replied that a business plan was prepared describing the business and the investment and then circulated to the right candidates. He knew of one retired executive who might be interested, adding cautiously that, of course, no guarantees could be made.

Oscar wondered how a business plan was prepared. Tim said there were books on the subject and companies that could write one for him. He said the first thing to do was to consult with his attorney and CPA on the process. Oscar didn't have any attorney or want one. He despised attorneys ever since he had been sued in an auto accident. Tim made the point that there were accident attorneys and there were business attorneys and that while one was trying to take your assets the other tried to grow and protect them. Oscar would have none of it, so Tim directed Oscar first to see his CPA to get the business plan started.

Oscar's CPA was really Larry the bookkeeper. Larry wasn't too familiar with the best means for conducting business but overcame this fundamental issue by being absolutely certain of his opinions. When Oscar visited Larry about preparing the business plan, Larry was certain about what to do. He told Oscar that he would continue as a sole proprietor and sell a 40% sole proprietorship interest to the new investor. Larry confidently indicated that he knew Oscar's business well enough and could write up the business plan for $5,000. Since Oscar had no idea how to do it, he let Larry proceed.

When the 9-page business plan was ready, Oscar called Tim about the potential investor. Tim wanted to see the plan, but was leaving town on vacation. He was well aware that Oscar needed the money and the help sooner rather than later. So he gave Oscar the address of the retired executive and had him forward the plan directly to him.

Two weeks passed and Oscar had heard nothing. He called Tim to see if there was any interest. Tim had forgotten about it all in the post-vacation crush of catch-up, but agreed to call the executive. Two hours later Tim called Oscar to have him come in and bring the plan with him.

Oscar arrived at the bank the next day wearing his best suit. He assumed he was going to meet the executive and his new business partner. But the scowl on Tim's face quickly ended that happy thought.

Tim angrily asked who had prepared the business plan. Oscar said Larry down on Railroad Avenue. Tim grimaced. Was Larry the bookkeeper Oscar's CPA?

Oscar asked what was wrong.

Tim was all too ready to vent. First of all, the 9-page business plan was sloppy, amateurish and incoherent in several places. It came nowhere near to providing the kind of serious, well thought out information a sophisticated investor wanted to see. Tim angrily noted that this awful document had reflected poorly on him. He had gone to bat for Oscar and put his reputation on the line for him. The executive now questioned Tim's judgment for allowing such a shoddy document to be presented. Referrals are risks. Tim took one for Oscar and it exploded in his face.

Tim continued to vent. An even bigger problem was that Oscar's plan still had the business held as a sole proprietorship. First of all, Tim had told Oscar a thousand times he needed to incorporate. The liability for a very active business such as his involving gas lines and repairs to expensive homes was too risky. And as a sole proprietor he could lose everything, including his business assets, his house and other personal assets. If he took the simple step of incorporating, he could protect his personal assets from being reached by a business creditor. Moreover, a serious investor looking at Oscar's business would have to conclude that Oscar was an idiot for operating as a sole proprietor. And investors don't invest with idiots.

Tim was really venting now. What was even more idiotic was that Larry had written in the plan that Oscar was selling a 40% sole proprietorship interest. It was at this point that Tim really blew. There was no such thing as a fractional sole proprietorship interest!

Only one person could own 100% of a sole proprietorship. You can't have more than one owner of a sole proprietorship. There are no partners in a sole proprietorship! What was Larry thinking? Did he even have one business brain cell?

Tim calmed himself. He asked Oscar why he thought Larry on the other side of the tracks could possibly give him correct legal advice. Oscar started to go on about attorneys but Tim angrily cut him off. It was time he got over this immature disdain of attorneys. He was a grown up entrepreneur and grown up entrepreneurs had business attorneys on their team. A business attorney would have never let this fiasco occur.

Oscar hung his head. Tim drove the point home. The bank could not continue to do business with Oscar if he didn't retain proper legal counsel. He needed to incorporate within two weeks or find a new bank.

Oscar left the office. Tim didn't hear from him. After ten days, Tim felt maybe had had been too hard on Oscar. He called him up to apologize and see how he was doing.

Oscar was in good spirits. He said he had met with a real CPA and a good business attorney. He reported that they were helping him straighten out the business and prepare a top-notch business plan. And Oscar thanked Tim for yelling at him. Only a friend would do that. And it was just what he needed to break through to the next level of business.

The lesson of this case is that structure is important. It matters to those reviewing your plan. Over ninety percent of all business plans will have their legal structure (be it a corporation, limited liability company or limited partnership) correctly in place and it won't be an issue.

But for the few entrepreneurs such as Oscar who haven't properly dealt with the important topic of limiting liability through the right entity, structure will be a huge issue. And unlike Tim, a friend who was vocal about what he saw, the wrong structure for many investors will be a silent decider. They won't tell you what was wrong with the plan, they'll just politely hand it back saying they have made other commitments. You'll never know that the real reason was that you made the cardinal (and very easily remedied) mistake of conducting business through a sole proprietorship or general partnership, neither of which offer asset protection to their owners.

A complete discussion of legal structures is beyond the scope of this book. You may want to read my book *Start Your Own Corporation* for a greater discussion of this important area.

While very important, the legal structure section of your business plan can be very basic. Begin with when the business was begun, and then move onto how the business was begun (include any licenses, contracts, agreements, charters, articles of incorporation, bylaws and the like in the Supporting Documents). Is your business a brand new startup or a purchase of an existing business or a franchise? If you are writing your business plan for a corporate expansion (which is an excellent idea), include all the facts from the original startup or purchase as well as those for the expansion phase.

The most basic description of your business (or business idea) is your choice of corporate entity. But a description is not enough. Potential investors and/or partners will want to know how you make decisions and why you make the choices you do. Your section on legal structure should include at least some discussion of why you chose the structure you did as well as why you set up your structure and terms of agreement as you did. This is also a good place to offer assurances. How do you plan to meet your corporate obligations? How will you maintain your corporate status? Do you have any plans to change your legal structure? And if so, how and why? Let your reader know you are mindful of the importance of legal structure and move on.

Business Description

The Business Description section is about the structure and strategy of your company. It should be a textual snapshot of your business, showing the primary activities of the business and how the business will make money.

Start with the basics. What type of business are you pursuing (manufacturing, service, retail, franchise, wholesale, etc.)? How many employees do you have in which departments? What is the product or service you offer? What is your market share (your net revenues divided by the net revenues of the industry)? What relationships do you have with suppliers, support businesses, customers, advertisers and the like? What resources (monetary and otherwise) do you currently have on hand for your business? How was the business established (startup, franchise, purchase, expansion)? Where is the business located? What are the business hours?

When describing your business, keep in mind the needs of the customer. Describe what problem you will solve for the consumer, what niche you will fill. The most impressive new gadget is worthless if it doesn't solve a problem. People don't generally spend money for products or services that do not fulfill some need. Even the Humvee, with its awkward size and abysmal gas mileage, fulfills the need of consumers who want to stand out. So your plan need not detail the inner-workings of your product (nor should it; remember that business plans tend to become public documents), but rather highlight the attraction of such a product or service to existing and potential customers. If your business solves more than one problem for more than one demographic, address both or all.

Once you have addressed what customer problem(s) you will solve and/or what niche you will fill, you are ready to address how you will translate that knowledge into a business. Don't worry about marketing here; save that for the Marketing section. For now, concentrate on what it is about your structure and strategy that will enable you to get your product or service ready for customers. Remember business structure and systems can often be a businesses competitive advantage. Great business plans highlights the advantages of each area of a business.

When describing your business, include pertinent information from the past, the present and the future. What is the company's history? What is its current status with regard to inventory, turnover, marketability, value? What changes are planned for the future and why? Are you planning any research and development activities? How do you see the business growing and changing over the next few years? What milestones can you see for the future? What opportunities await you? What risks do you foresee and how will you prepare for them?

Part of this section deals with future plans, so take some space to discuss your business goals. Explain how you will meet these goals, what changes will be necessary, what plans you have, how you are already laying the groundwork to meet future goals. This is the place to discuss how you will not only keep your business going, but how your business will improve over time. Do you have plans for acquisitions or expansions? If so, when? You might want to include some information on how you are already planning for future events that may present risks or opportunities to your business. Include a timeline that stretches out a few years.

The Business Description section may also include an overview of your organizational structure, which is important because you want to take every opportunity to reinforce the experience, education and track record of your team. Don't worry about great detail here, however. You'll have the Management and Personnel subsection for that. For now, your organization structure may be as simple as an organizational chart. Include the ownership and management of the top two or three levels for the company as a whole as well as within departments. You may want to keep it to department names and personnel titles only or you may want to include employee names. You may want to add more detail and give a brief description of each department (necessary if you're structure is not common or intuitive) and brief job descriptions of owners and management. If management and ownership consists of just you at the moment, say so.

The more important your organizational team is to your business' success, the more detail you should include. If it is the individual skills of your management team that gives you a competitive edge, go ahead and include some of those skills in this section. If you have no management lined up, just include titles and perhaps basic job descriptions. If you are planning on that structure changing over the short run, you may want to be more vague, perhaps leaving out job descriptions altogether. The same goes for department descriptions.

If your departmental structure is unique, offers an edge, or simply proves how well you have thought through your business, give it some detail. If you know that the departmental structure will be changing, go ahead and discuss those changes. Include a timeline for clarity. Don't be afraid of change. Let your knowledge of your company's future show that you have really thought things through and that you have a firm understanding of your business and industry.

Depending on your business, some possible departments to discuss or at least outline include the following:

- Franchise
- Research and Development
- Manufacturing
- Inventory, Warehousing or Storage
- Transportation
- Purchasing
- Sales
- Marketing
- Customer Service
- Information Technology

- Finances and Accounting
- Human Resources
- Facilities

Include whatever sections apply to your business, but put the most important ones first. It is a reality of our society that we lack patience and we are all busier than we'd like. Readers will want to get through your plan as quickly as possible. They may skip sections. Putting the important sections first decreases the chances of your audience missing important information. Or, as they say in some parts, "Don't hide your light under a bushel."

Every section of the plan is an opportunity to prove yourself and your ideas. Use the Business Description subsection to show your knowledge of the industry and your market and how your product or service fits into both. This is an excellent place to list business strengths and weaknesses, though it is not the only section in which to include such information. It is an especially good place to introduce the uniqueness of your product or service because such uniqueness should be a cornerstone of your entire business.

Remember, what makes your business strong will likely be a function of:
- the quality, experience and passion of your people
- your ability to focus on cash flow
- your ability to create distinctive business systems
- the uniqueness of the product or service,
- how the product or service is different from others in the market,
- price and/or
- relationships

Do you have an edge when it comes to business relationships? Will you be courting government contracts? What expertise, relationships or experience do you have that will facilitate your landing such jobs?

If you're in business to make money, (and certainly your investors will hope that you are), how exactly do you plan to do so? Your plan should give an overview of potential revenue streams. Include details such as pricing, costs, discounts (if any), type and cost of sales force, kinds and amount of marketing and everything you know about sales cycles in your industry. Include information on all pertinent revenue streams. For example, if your office supply store also offers technology consultation, you have at least two separate revenue streams. Indicate how much of overall revenues each income stream is responsible for and what margins (gross or operational) you can expect from each.

Clearly identify the initial cash investment necessary to start the business along with each major bucket of spending as well as describe the cash flow needs of the business throughout its startup. Most novice entrepreneurs confuse profitability with cash flow. If a business is growing rapidly it can get caught without enough cash for inventory, which creates serious issues for original investors who can get "crammed down" by new lenders or investors who are brought in to save the day for a growing but poorly managed enterprise.

Again, not all business plans are, or should be, for the purpose of raising capital. Business plans are an excellent management tool. As such, you may want to share your plan with management and other personnel. However, though you may choose to use your plan for management purposes, you don't have to share every aspect of the plan. You may have information you want to keep private (salaries, proprietary information, corporate weaknesses). Then again, maybe you want full knowledge for all employees. An open book policy works for some businesses.

In this Business Description subsection, you have an opportunity to let partners and employees know how their hard work will pay off. While some owners do not relish the thought of letting employees in on the details of the business (especially details of revenue), this kind of information can be a great incentive. Unless your business is dumping truckloads of cash on the front porches of owners/partners/shareholders, your employees are likely to be surprised to see the narrow margins under which most businesses struggle. They may not fully realize how much it costs to keep the doors open every month. These issues, as described in your plan, can take the emphasis off you as owner and put it back on the benefits to employees.

Take some space in your plan to show that you are thinking of the future for your employees as well as for yourself. Show how money will be put back into the business in the form of better facilities, better benefits, increased numbers of employees and the like. Let your employees feel they have a stake in your business and ideally you will engender a loyal workforce, thereby decreasing turnover and cutting training costs.

Product or Service Description

In the Business Description subsection, you address strategy and structure. In the Product or Service Description subsection, you address the process by which you execute that strategy. From materials through production to finished product, from bid through proposal to completed project, any steps taken to get your product or service before the customer should be listed in this subsection.

There are many questions to answer in this subsection, but you still have to keep it short. You don't want readers to be tempted to skim; they may miss that pertinent detail that makes your company viable and unique.

Don't get overly technical. Remember that your audience is not likely at the same level of expertise as you. Nor do they care to be. Most readers of your plans are more interested in whether or not you can make money off your idea than they are in the gee-whiz hoopla of your product. Obviously a managerial business plan can include more detail as to the niftiness of the product, service or operation than a plan designed to attract capital.

Rich Dad Tips

- At this point in the process, recognize how much has been covered and how overwhelming writing a plan can appear. Break the process into smaller pieces and don't try to complete everything at once. Remember, great entrepreneurs have the ability to delay immediate gratification. Building a successful business is hard work and creating a winning plan is no exception.

- The business plan is where inspiration meets perspiration. This process is a great "gut-check" to see just how motivated you are to truly live your dreams. This section is tedious and detailed for most entrepreneurial spirits, but it is absolutely necessary and must be given considerable attention and forethought. Don't rush the plan no matter how impatient you become.

When you are writing the Product or Service subsection, consider what product you offer. (Remember that if you are writing the plan for a service business, the service is the product). Discuss any research and development that might be needed to bring your product to market. Do you have any patents or patents pending or trademarks on your products or services? How are products made and by whom? Include flowcharts or a discussion of key processes within the company. Don't give away any trade secrets, but be sure that your audience can tell how things get done within the structure you have established, or plan to establish.

Discuss product specifics. Are products built to order or built for inventory? From fabrication to assembly to inspection, show how a product goes from development to sale. Depending on your business, you may be looking at welding, wiring, machining, molding, food preparation, stocking inventory, inventory control -- it's all process. What materials do you require to produce the product? Where do you get the materials? Give the location and company names of such suppliers. Will you have freight costs? If so, when and how much?

Many businesses require capital equipment—cars, machines, computers and more. What equipment needs do you foresee for your business? Think it through and be prepared for a discussion, not just a list. Why do you need the capital equipment and when will you need it? What costs will you have associated with capital equipment? Don't forget about installation, maintenance, repair and replacement. Have you accounted for depreciation in your financial projections? Any business plan should include an equipment list. Let yours show that you understand the current and future needs of your business.

People make a business go, but your business is made up of more than just the people who work under your roof. Vendors and suppliers have more of an impact on your business than you might at first think. As you grow in your business you will come to appreciate how much these relationships can mean. Your investors already know this. So address this section with seriousness. How did you come to choose the suppliers or vendors you use? How long have you had a relationship with suppliers or vendors and what kind of agreements do you have with them? How do you pay vendors or suppliers? Is it by check, credit and/or cash?

Consider the level of quality of raw materials and how that quality could affect the quality of your product. What assurances do you have from suppliers or vendors as to product quality?

Supplier and vendor costs affect your profit. What discounts are offered and under what circumstances? What are your major raw materials or costs? Do costs fluctuate? If so, how do you plan to prepare yourself for swings in raw material costs?

Supplier and vendor capabilities could affect your level of output. How will you handle increases or decreases in production? Whether due to a sudden economic change or just a soured relationship, you may be forced to jump quickly. Do you have backup suppliers or vendors in mind?

Most businesses keep more product than just that seen by potential customers at any given time. As such, you'll need to discuss your inventory. How much do you need? How much do you have? Where do you keep your inventory? How do you track inventory?

Facilities are critical for businesses that are more than just office-based. But don't discount the importance of office space either. Discuss your needs regarding space, layout (include a basic floor plan with work flow indicated), expandability, startup costs and operating costs. Discuss how you will acquire facilities, whether by lease, purchase, build-out, conversion, or new build. Articulate when they will be needed and what they will cost. Give the contract basics, including not only costs, but also terms. Will the facilities require renovations? If so, what kinds and when?

If you plan to start a service business, discuss what services you will offer. What will you charge and under what terms? How did you arrive at your pricing plan? Will services be performed at your site or will you go to the client? What geographical area will you serve? Who does the actual work (staff or contractors)? Where will you find employees? How will you attract employees with the right skills? Will you use subcontractors? How much work will be done in-house, how much will be contracted out? What services will be handled in-house, what will be contracted out? What equipment does the service require? What agreements do you have with vendors? How did you choose vendors? How long have you had relationships with vendors? What discounts can you expect and under what circumstances? What discounts will you offer and under what circumstances? What do the services cost? How will you handle increases and decreases in workload? What hours will service be available?

Whether your business is service-based or product-based, failure to find the right personnel for the job may be a deal breaker for your plan. Again, your investors know this. If you are trying to start a software development business in rural Mississippi, rural Montana, or rural anywhere, you are going to have to overcome a huge hurdle in terms of a technically skilled and available labor pool. In all cases you must present a logical plan that details what personnel is needed, where they will be recruited from, and when various positions will need to be filled. Disclose how you will go about getting the right people for the right job at the right time. Discuss whether or not suitable labor is available locally. If suitable labor can be recruited, how will it be recruited? Where will labor most likely come from and will you offer training? If so, what kind and for how long? What pay will you offer to in-house personnel, contractors and trainees? What benefits will you offer and under what terms?

Put some thought into product quality, warranty and customer service after the sale. Do you offer any warranty on products? Do you offer any product service after the sale? If you do offer service or warranties, what are the terms? Where will necessary repairs or other service be performed and will such work be performed in house or contracted out?

If you have more than one product, discuss both (or all). If you offer products and services, discuss both (or all). If you are planning changes or additions to your products or services, include that information along with details as to how and when you are planning to change.

Similarly, include a discussion about information technology that is important to your business. Recall that information technology used to be called hardware and software, and before that computers and programs. Even if you are using an abacus and crayons, you have to deal with how the business processes information. Think through what systems you need. If you retain an information technology consultant to assess your needs, be careful as to whether they are on a commission for product sales. You want to be lean and effective, not overburdened with expensive computer items that will be outmoded in three years. That said, include a paragraph (or more if necessary to your business) on how you will deal with all of the information technology issues. This is another area that novices typically underestimate the cost and energy necessary to compete in a world with rapidly advancing technology. What is an advantage today could be gone by tomorrow if a competitor trumps you with technology.

The timing of your business may be another important factor. Laying out a graph or timelines for acquisitions, research, development, renovations, introduction of new products or services, hiring, and the like while also showing in what order things need to happen is helpful for management or investors. It's a good way to plan the basics of your business -- a way to set out sub-goals that lead to larger goals that lead to success.

The Product or Service Description subsection is another common area in which to include your strengths and weaknesses. If it is your product or service that differentiates you from the competition, explain so in this section. If your product or service is new, you will need more detail than if it is a variation on an existing form of business.

While we have mentioned it before, again think about what it is that encourages customers to purchase your product. What sets your product or service apart from that of the competition? Do you offer an innovative solution to a problem? Is it your price that differentiates your product or service? Is your product less expensive or do you offer shipping incentives? Is variety your strong point? Do you offer more options to personalize the product or service or even more options as to where to get the product or service? Do you offer a comprehensive or innovative service plan? Are you quicker than the competition? What other incentives do you offer?

Whatever you can include in your plan that will show your product or service as not only different but also superior to that of the competition will help you in reaching your goals.

Investors typically only give you money for a piece of a business they think is going to offer strong returns. Bankers are more likely to take a risk and loan you money if they think your product or service will sell. Your management will go more smoothly if employees and advertisers can see what it is you are truly trying to sell. And what you are truly trying to sell is the differences between you and the rest of the herd, which need to be relevant to your customers as well.

Of course, the differences have to be real and they have to make a difference to the bottom line. Remember that what counts on the bottom line is increasing revenues and/or decreasing costs. If the competition offers four colors of staplers and you offer six, that's really not a big enough difference to sell your plan — from a financial or management perspective. But if you offer a stapler that runs on a remote control and leaves no visible mark, you might be onto something. Be creative when thinking through your business, your products and/or your services -- but be realistic and honest on the page. A winning business plan is one that conveys, above all else, honesty.

Intellectual Property Description

Karen and Roger

Karen had written an excellent business plan for her new business. She was going to sell quality pearls from Hawaii and the South Pacific direct to consumers over the Internet, saving them hundreds, if not thousands of dollars, in the process. Her suppliers were lined up, the web site was ready to launch. All she needed was $100,000 for advertising and working capital. Her use of funds in the business plan was clearly detailed.

Roger was a sophisticated investor. He had done well getting in early on cash flow business ventures. He knew this company wouldn't go public but could be sold in several years for a handsome profit to another company. He was initially interested in the idea.

For Roger a key feature of any business was the intellectual property rights. Anyone could, for example, set up a business to sell pearls over the Internet. There weren't that many barriers to entering the business. Instead, what allowed entrepreneurs to stake their claim and protect their turf were trademarks and Internet domain names. Once they were in place and proper marketing and brand building had begun, a barrier to entry by potential competitors could be erected.

In the world of business plans there are some specific sections that certain people read first. Lawyers go to the litigation section. Executives want to read the management section to see how the executive team stacks up. The first thing Roger looked at in a business plan was the discussion of intellectual property. For him trademarks, copyrights and patents were the most important assets a business had to offer.

Karen's section on intellectual property described the domain names she had secured. But it didn't discuss any trademarks. This got Roger wondering about her situation.

Karen's main domain name was a good one: clear, easy to remember and sure to naturally drive traffic to her site. But when Roger did an online trademark search he learned that another company already had the trademark for the same name.

Roger knew this presented a major problem. Under federal law, a trademark can trump a domain name. If a company has a preexisting trademark registration, it can force an independent party that managed to register their trademark as a domain name to turn over the domain name. That was the case here. It was clear that Karen's use of the great domain name would soon invite legal demands and perhaps litigation. A new business didn't need such problems.

For Roger, a lack of understanding of the importance of intellectual property indicated a deficiency in overall management skills. As such, in his opinion, the future success of the company was diminished. Without ever telling Karen why, Roger declined to invest.

If intellectual property is important to your business, which is increasingly the case, you will need to discuss it in your business plan. Intellectual property includes copyrights, patents, trademarks, domain names and trade secrets. If you have the rights already, great, say so. If there are rights you need, but have not acquired, outline the timeline of the acquisition process and note how far along you are in that process. Of course, this is a risky proposition. Many potential investors will not turn past this page if you do not have the proper rights in place. The risk is too great. And it's all about risk. As such, you may want to secure domain names and file for patents and trademarks before you put forth the plan for review. Equally important, you should think about and include a brief discussion as to how you will protect the intellectual property rights you do have.

Rich Dad Tips

- An intellectual property attorney should review all of your intellectual proprety to ensure it is either usable or ownable and doesn't infringe on others rights. You don't want to be surprised by a cease and desist letter from a major corporation.

- Remember that once released, your business plan is a public document that can be reproduced and read by others who you may not want to see it.

- There is nothing to prevent these unwanted viewers from filing for your intellectual property rights ahead of you. It is strongly suggested that you file for all available rights before you distribute your business plan.

Litigation

If you have been sued or threatened with a suit, you must disclose this in the litigation section. Likewise, if your company has initiated legal proceedings it must be disclosed. This may seem like a very difficult subject to write about. Who wants to invest in a company that is being sued?

But litigation and lawyers are now a permanent part of the business landscape. Some entrepreneurs, companies, and even real estate investors focus on their legal strategy as much as they do on marketing. Sophisticated investors understand this and will not be deterred by the presence of litigation that occurs in the ordinary course of business. That said, investors could have second thoughts about investing if the result of the litigation could snuff out the company's survivability, such as an environmental or hazardous waste claim or the inability to use a key technology or proprietary process. But also know that failing to disclose such a material matter as litigation can give those same investors a claim against you personally for misrepresentation and fraud. When in doubt, disclose. On the other hand, if you are free from such issues, you will have the luxury of writing the following:

Litigation
The company is not currently engaged in or threatened with any
litigation or other legal proceedings.

Location

Location is not necessarily a critical factor for all businesses, but it should be discussed in all business plans. Where to include this subsection is a matter of how location affects your business. If location is a marketing component (your office supply store is located in the heart of the business district, for example), put the Location subsection in the Marketing section. If location is a simple business component, include the Location subsection in the Business section.

Discussion of location should begin with the basics -- where the business is located (address), how it is zoned, why the particular location was chosen (nearness of shipping facilities and/or supplies, ease for target market, cost) and what facilities are at the location. Then expand on each. Include a physical description (with square footage) of the site along with the name of a contact person (such as a Realtor) and the cost of the site. Bring in some history: the history of the site (especially in regards to possible and problematic hazardous waste) and some history on why you chose the site and what other locations were considered. Do you have enough parking? (Include parking in your diagram of the site) In the Supporting Documents, you may want to include any lease agreements and photos or drawings of the site.

The area surrounding and servicing your location is also important to your business' future success, and, as such, should be addressed in your plan. What is the business climate in the area? What kind of businesses already exist in the area and will you be competing with them? Are there any foreseeable trends that might affect your choice of location or its desirability? What is the local labor force like and will it be able to meet your needs? What are local salaries like? Is there adequate housing for your labor force? What is the local crime rate and, if your business will be open after dark, is there sufficient lighting? How are the public services? Is there adequate police and fire protection? Are public utilities up to your standards and will they be able to absorb your use, as well as future expansions? If customers will be coming to the site, how is traffic for those customers? If you will be dealing with shipping (in or out), what is the ease of shipping by rail, road or air?

Don't forget about the future. If everything goes well, will your location allow for expansion? If things do not go well, will your location be conducive to downsizing? Address all the factors that go into such expansions or contractions of your business -- personnel, buildings, land, parking, traffic, zoning, lease agreements and the like.

By focusing on the structure and strategy of your business or real estate project, you will go a long way towards preparing a solid, readable and winning business plan.

Chapter Nine

The Logistics

"The secret of all victory lies in the organization of the nonobvious."
– Oswald Spengler

L ogistics, like structure and strategy, are another important element of the winning business plan. All operational details must be carried out efficiently and effectively for the business to succeed.

Have you ever thought about all the steps to be followed and details to be covered by UPS or FedEx when they pick up and deliver a package? On the surface it looks seamless. They pick it up and your client gets it the next day. Behind the scenes there are many people doing a very large number of specific tasks to get it all done.

Your business will be unique but in all businesses there are logistical functions to deal with.

Many of these functions will not be apparent to your customers. They will most certainly be important to your investors. In this chapter, we'll discuss the key logistical topics to be addressed in your business plan.

Management and Personnel

Personnel is one of the most important elements of the business plan. Sam Walton, founder of Wal-Mart said, "I don't care what business you're in, you're in the business of people." Great entrepreneurs and savvy investors know the first place to look in an investment is the quality of the company's management team. Investors and lenders look to management's experience, education and track record of success in rewarding investors and/or paying down debt. Money follows good management and this is your opportunity to shine.

Frank and Brooke

Frank and Brooke were planning to open a real estate brokerage business. Frank had been a real estate agent in town for 15 years and had just obtained his broker's license. He knew the market, got around town and had a good local following.

Brooke was a sales agent and a rising star in the real estate community. In three years she had scored some impressive listings and had closed a number of significant deals.

Together they hoped to make quite a team.

While they had enough money to open a basic office, both Frank and Brooke recognized that they needed to write a business plan to appreciate exactly what they were getting into. They knew it would force them to focus on logistics--the necessary operational details key to business success.

For Frank, the plan needed to detail how many people they would need to run the office. At his old firm, the boss was not dedicated to the bottom line and had too many people on the payroll. The big commissions checks came in and everyone seemed to get paid, whether they were 100% productive or not. Frank wanted to run a tighter ship.

Brooke wanted to make sure all the bases were covered. She did what she did best, sell. She didn't want to be burdened by the logistics of running an office. It had to be done. It had to be seamless. But the secretarial and accounting tasks would have to be performed by someone else if she was to excel.

So with the forces of payroll cost reduction and necessary personnel requirements at work, Frank and Brooke sat down to discuss what was needed and what was not.

Both of them agreed that a bookkeeper was necessary. The accounting, and especially the tracking of monies held in trust, was crucial. Frank had spoken to their CPA, who suggested that an outside bookkeeping firm be utilized until it was necessary to hire an in-house bookkeeper.

Secretarial support was a must. At the start they needed a competent staffer who could answer the phone, type a letter, get out the packages and handle administrative details. Brooke suggested that this person be paid a little more than the average receptionist or secretary and be groomed to be a future office manager. As the firm grew so would their role and compensation. Brooke argued it was important for them to have an administrative all star on board with them at the start, and that it was worth an extra $2 an hour for such a person. Frank grudgingly agreed.

In terms of management, as a broker Frank was required by the state's real estate laws to manage the office. Because they had decided to operate as an S corporation with Frank as President, Brooke as secretary/treasurer and both of them as directors, the corporate management was the two of them. They agreed that extra management personnel were not needed at this time. Since they were small, the necessary tasks of human resources (hiring, firing and training) as well as sales and marketing would be handed by the two of them.

Computers, or information technology as consultants like to call it to justify higher fees, were a necessary part of any business. Neither Frank nor Brooke had a clue about them. Still, they did not see a need for an in-house person to handle these issues. Brooke knew several computer services from her various lead groups and agreed to check into pricing.

As Frank and Brooke continued to talk it appeared that a number of the related services, such as legal and financial should all be outsourced at the start. And so it came down to the need for one well qualified and, at Brooke's insistence, decently paid administrative staffer to get the firm going.

Frank and Brooke agreed the discussion was beneficial. Not only had they decided what they did and didn't need, but they had created a specific job description and identity for the one employee they needed to move forward.

While the Management and Personnel subsection will not be long or detailed, you will need to do some preliminary work before you can start the section. The first thing you will need to do is an analysis of what skills and tasks are or will be needed to make the business go. Your research into your industry and competition should give you a list of skills necessary.

Some common skills are:

Bookkeeping	Legal
Accounting	Interpersonal communication
Financial planning	Customer service
Human resources	Project management
Management	Vision
Leadership	Goal setting
Sales	Strategizing
Marketing	Banking
Information technology	Pricing
Security	Politics
Safety	Regulations
Insurance	Analysis of business trends
Time management	Market identification and segmentation
Organization	
Real estate	Training
Construction/contracting	

Depending on your business, you may also need experience in:

Research	Inventory tracking
Development	Transportation and shipping
Production	Repair
Distribution	

Every business has its own set of skill requirements. Retail is vastly different from manufacturing; construction is light years from consulting.

If you don't know what skills are necessary to your chosen business, you may have chosen the wrong business.

Be sure you know all the skill needs of your business and then move on to the actual tasks that will need to be performed, from welding to food storage, calculating sales tax to calculating carrying capacity. Get a stack of index cards and start writing out one skill or task (or both) per card until you have covered all the categories you can possibly think of that will be needed for the running of your business. Some of the skills and/or tasks will be needed daily, some weekly, some monthly, some yearly. Note this cyclical nature on each card. Be as specific as you can. Do you need to know how to handle transportation by rail or by road or both? Can bookkeeping be performed on a weekly or biweekly basis? (You may be surprised to learn that it will be a daily need.) Estimate how long it will take to perform every task (by day, week, month or year) listed on each card. Now double each number, knowing that we all tend to radically underestimate how much time it will take to perform a task, any task.

Next rate your skill level as strong, adequate or weak for each category (card) and separate out the categories you feel you are strong in. Add up all the time estimates. You will now have a good idea of whether or not you will have time to perform just the tasks that play to your strengths.

If your stack of strengths leaves extra time, separate out the cards for the skills at which you rated yourself as adequate. Stack these cards according to your level of strength or by the level of income you would have to pay someone else.

Taking into account the number of hours you are willing to put into the business each week, you should be able to see what areas will require added personnel. Rearrange the remaining cards either by their level of importance to the business or by the amount it will cost you to hire someone to perform that skill. Keep working with the cards until you have a good idea of your personnel needs and costs for startup as well as for the future.

You may want to organize the cards by job description and start putting down names of possible employees. Or you may choose to organize cards according to personnel or partners you have lined up already.

Finally, if you haven't done so already, you can use your cards to plan out your organizational structure. With cards categorized by employee, partner or job description, you can group together those jobs that logically work together. From there you can choose management by person or skill set.

You should now be ready to begin the Management and Personnel subsection of your plan. While you won't need to include a detailed description of every single position in the business, you will need to list the positions in a summary of your organizational structure, whether in text or by charts.

You will need to include information on the key players in your business -- principals and management. Save the complete resumes for the Supporting Documents, but do include a brief job description (be as precise as you can) and a very brief (think one paragraph) summary of the pertinent experience of each member of the owner and/or management team. This experience will likely be primarily business experience, but if that is lacking, don't hesitate to include other experience, such as life experience or skills gained through hobbies or volunteer work, that show your team members can handle their jobs. Readers will want to know how the background of principals and management will help the business, so show them.

Rich Dad Tips

- Appreciate that the Management and Personnel section will be one of the most frequently read sections of your plan. It will be on the top-three list for most readers. Knowing this, write the section clearly and persuasively to accentuate the strengths of management.

- One reason for the section's popularity has to do with its People Magazine/gossip style nature. People want to read about what other people are doing. Consider including personal information such as unique accomplishments, educational background, and family status (i.e. wife and kids) to make this section interesting to the reader.

As you write this section, discuss current personnel needs as well as those you see in the near future (three to five years). Flesh out some of the information you highlighted in the Product or Service Description section to give readers a firm handle on your personnel needs and your ability to meet those needs. Include information on what level of training employees will need, whether you will offer that training or pay for it. Discuss where you will find employees. Provide a timeline for when personnel will need to be added. What hours will employees work? What will be your typical work schedule for the first year by week and by month? What will employees be paid and what will employees cost you, including wages, salaries, benefits and taxes? What benefits will you offer employees and when will they be eligible?

Most businesses find themselves needing expertise, but do not always need to add staff to meet those needs. Think about where you can use subcontractors and where you might be able to hire people on a per project basis. Consider how you will handle accounting, legal, banking, insurance and the like. Will you put professionals on retainer or pay an hourly fee? Include the reasons for your choices as well as the terms of your agreements. Show that you are ready to handle all the organizational issues like an experienced veteran.

Don't be afraid of weaknesses. Everyone has weaknesses. No one knows everything and your readers know this. You will have likely included your team members' strengths in their experience summaries. Now use a discussion of your weaknesses, as well as those of pertinent members of your management team, to once again show your business savvy. Explain what areas you foresee as troublesome and explain what you plan to do to compensate. By raising a concern and then quickly alleviating that concern you are able to show your honesty and your foresight as well as your in-depth understanding of your industry and your business' unique needs.

If you are writing a business plan for an existing business, don't overlook your partners and employees as a valuable resource. Consider having partners and employees write their own job descriptions. Not only will this take some work off your hands, it can help you make sure that everyone has the same understanding of their duties. Also take the time to talk to partners and employees about every other aspect of the plan. You might be surprised by the perspectives and valuable input of others who work with and for you.

Include in your plan the steps you take to ensure that employees buy into your decision-making and that they are able to bring their ideas for improvements and changes to you. If this relationship does not exist, think about why it doesn't. Depending on your answers you may or may not want to include such information. If you ask the question and your honest answer has to do with ego rather than an efficient, intentional management system, you might want to rethink your management style.

If you are writing your plan for a franchise, include a subsection on franchise help. In addition to yourself and your employees, there should be a whole system in place to help you get up and going and achieve success. Describe the help that will be available to you (include manuals and the like) as well as how long you will have access to management help after startup.

Records

Logistics includes the management of information. All the information in the world is useless if you can't get to it when you need it. This section of your business plan (as with all the others) should show that you are efficient and organized and have a strong understanding of your business' needs. Discuss what recordkeeping system or service you have chosen and why. Do the same for accounting. Which will you use and why? Will bookkeeping and accounting be done on-site, off-site, or a combination of both? Who will be responsible for records and accounts and do you have personnel proficient in analysis of financial records? Show how you will use recordkeeping and/or bookkeeping to improve your business, be it through the systems you use or through making choices based on the results of those systems.

Give some thought to the security of your records. Where will files be stored? What sort of security measures will you have for records? How important is proprietary information to your business? How will you protect such information? Which employees will have access to what records? How long will records be kept and how will records be disposed of and by whom?

Different business will have different records to keep and different record protection needs. Be sure you understand yours and show that you can handle the load.

Insurance

Every business is liable to have liability. Your goals should be not only to keep your liability to a minimum but also to prove to potential investors that you recognize the realities of product and personal liabilities in your industry. This knowledge will help you lay the groundwork to prove that you are not a high risk to investors. Investors want to see a return on their investments. They do not want to see their investment be sucked down into the mire of a preventable lawsuit, or any other kind of lawsuit, for that matter.

Businesses that sell a product need to prepare for product liability considerations. Even the highest quality product may break, and if it does, you may be liable. How will you handle it? What coverage will you need? Talk to your insurance broker about a risk assessment review to make sure you are properly covered.

Businesses that sell a service need to prepare for personal liability considerations. You need to provide insurance for the property of your clients while that property is under your care. Whether the property is sitting in your warehouse, being repaired in your service bay or being transported from one place to another, it is your responsibility to make sure the property is safe and sound.

Obviously, if your business sells both products and services (and many do these days), you will need to be sure you are covered for both product and personal liability.

If you will be having non-employees (such as customers) on site, you will need to protect the safety of those people as well as your investment. (Yes, you will have to protect employees as well; read on.) Check into both public liability and property damage insurance.

If you have any employees, you will need to have insurance -- employee benefits as well as liability coverage. Will you offer medical, dental, prescription or even mental health insurance? In competitive labor markets, your benefit plan may be your ticket to finding and keeping qualified employees. But you will also need to offer employees protection on the job. Worker's compensation insurance is not optional. If one of your employees injures him or herself on the job, the company is liable. This doesn't just apply to high-risk industries such as manufacturing or construction. Even office workers can get injured on the job -- think, repetitive stress injuries for starters. Be sure you have adequate insurance coverage, some of which is required by law anyway.

If you lease property, buildings or equipment, your lease agreement may have its own requirements for insurance. Be sure to include these agreements in your Insurance subsection. If you anticipate you will be leasing property, buildings or equipment, be sure you know what insurance is required in standard agreements and address your plans for acquiring appropriate coverage.

Unless you are in the insurance business, it is best to sit down and have a one-on-one with an insurance agent to be sure all your proverbial bases are covered. If you use a vehicle for company use, make sure your insurance covers it. Get property insurance for any business property or facilities you own. What will happen if a partner dies? Life insurance needs to take into account partnerships and business ownership. Does your industry require bonding? Discuss what insurance you have or will have (and when) along with how long it is good for. Give some reasons as to why you decided on the carrier(s) and plan(s) you chose.

As always, do some preliminary research. Though you will hopefully hire experts you can trust, you should still not go into money matters blind. Know the industry standards for insurance. Don't let a good salesman convince you that you need more insurance than you really do.

Security

Security is another area that has direct bearing on your level of risk. If you have property, you run the risk of damage. If you have products or supplies, you run the risk of both damage and theft. If you have information, you run the risk of theft or leaks. Understand the security needs of your business and be ready to show you are willing and able to reduce those risks.

Not all employees are or will be completely honest. Sometimes the temptation of taking property or information is too great to resist. Do yourself and your employees a favor by decreasing temptation through appropriate and effective security. This may mean security personnel, surveillance cameras, security technology, insurance, property enhancements, training or other measures.

The Security subsection of your business plan should address how you plan to deal with the potential of theft (whether that theft is of computers, inventory, money, sensitive documents, etc.), damage and/or injury for your property and employees. This is another one of those pesky areas where it pays to know your business (or potential business) inside and out before you even start writing your plan. What areas in your industry are sensitive to theft or damage? What are the standards of security in your industry? Then you can go into the hows and whys of your security plans. How will you protect property, information and personnel within your company? Why did you choose the plan you will implement? What difference will your security plans make in the protection of your company?

Again, unless you are an insurance expert, sit down with a qualified insurance agent to help you map out your security measures. You may find you are eligible for rate discounts based on your security steps.

In addition, you may choose to consult with security experts in your field or even hire staff for ongoing security expertise. It depends on the particular needs of your business. You may just need a padlock on the front door or you may need a top-of-the-line, high tech security system rivaling that found in the latest blockbuster movie. Plan for your security needs now. Talking to the police after a theft is not the time to realize there are holes in your security plan.

The logistics -- the operational mastery of personnel, insurance, record keeping and similar details -- is an important part of your plan. Conversely, overlooking the logistics because they aren't revenue-exciting elements is a mistake. Succeeding at logistics is what makes you money and sets you apart. Investors well know this to be true. A winning business plan covers these issues thoroughly.

Chapter Ten

Marketing Your Business

*"Of all human powers operating on the affairs of mankind,
none is greater than that of competition."*
– Henry Clay

The Marketing

Marketing is another major element in any business plan. It includes identifying appropriate markets and customers, getting to know the competition, planning for efficient and effective distribution, establishing relationships (with distributors, sales staff, advertisers, customers, and the like), identifying and implementing appropriate advertising, awareness of industry and market trends and finding the perfect strategy for your business, including pricing, packaging and positioning. Marketing is the systematic process that inspires targeted customers to take action and buy your product and service.

Marketing is obviously more than just an ad campaign. Marketing relates to every aspect of your business. From the design of your package to the conduct of your sales staff to the promptness of delivery to the efficiency of your customer service -- everyone who works for you is involved with marketing because everyone is involved with making the sale. Your business lives and dies on sales. Your employees owe their jobs to those sales. They must be energetic. A salesman minus enthusiasm is just a clerk. Everyone in the company needs to remember that bottom-line reality. Blair Singer writes about this important issue in *Team Code of Honor.* Everyone must be selling.

As with The Business section, begin The Marketing section with a one-page overview of your marketing plan. Each aspect in your summary should be fleshed out within the subsections to follow. Include pertinent supporting information and data in the Supporting Documents. Think past, present and future. What have you done in the past? Include your experience and that of your staff, past marketing approaches, historic indicators in the field and useful relationships. What are you doing now? Discuss the ways you are staying abreast of industry and market trends, how you are using relationships and how you are currently getting your message to customers. What will you do in the future? Review how you will build upon your successes and learn from your failures. How will you make your message and your brand even more powerful?

Markets

Markets are usually described in two ways: buyers and dollars. In terms of buyers, your market encompasses all the people who might potentially pay for your product or service. Admittedly, this is probably an unwieldy group to even comprehend. For that reason, the Markets subsection of your plan should start with a description of the overall potential (or real) market and then work into a more manageable discussion of target markets.

Start with who will purchase your product or service. Explain why this group (or groups) would be interested in your product or service. (Keep in mind that your potential customers may not know that they would be interested in your products or services. They may not even know why they need your products or services.) To narrow that group down, consider why these consumers would choose your company as the supplier of that product or service rather than another company. There may be more than one reason and thus more than one market. Is it quality, advertising, ease, distance or price that attracts customers? Different groups will find different aspects appealing. The key for you is to find characteristics shared by each group.

When it comes to identifying target markets, think in terms of demographics (age, sex, family size, income, occupation, race, religion, and region), psychographics (needs, interests, attitudes, and lifestyles) and industrial demographics (SIC code, location, net worth, employee numbers, and sales). Ask as many questions as you can think of. What is the average age, income level and education level of this group? What is the gender makeup? Where do they live? Once you have identified the similarities you have developed a target market. You can take the customers you know of (or can reasonably expect) and start looking for other customers who share the characteristics of the existing group.

In terms of dollars, what is the size of the current market? How much of that market can you hope to capture and how. (Do not skip the "how.") How is the overall market expected to grow during that same time period? How quickly is it currently growing? Is it growing at all? If your business is involved with several markets, break each out by relative size according to sales. Once you have rated markets by dollar inputs, try breaking down your markets into target markets according to demographics. This will give you a better handle on how much each target might represent in sales for you.

So now you know how big your markets are in terms of customers and dollars. Break it down even more. What do the members of each group buy? Not just in your industry but in others as well. With this information, you can extrapolate what elements consumers are looking for: quality, price, customization, and location. Estimate the high end and low end for these elements -- what price range sells well, what level of quality do consumers expect. Find out how much each group contributes per capita in order to figure out which target markets might bring you the best profit margin. Now you can prioritize your markets and figure out where to best spend your marketing dollars.

Once you have determined the pertinent facts about your target markets, consider how those markets may change over time. As the overall population grows, will your market? If so, how? If not, how will you compensate? If a market were to fall away, are there opportunities for new markets? Discuss the social issues that could affect your business in the future, such as the increase in telecommuters, later average retirement ages or increased single-parent households. Explain how you will use this information to improve your bottom line.

Obviously the identification of markets and, more specifically, target markets, takes research -- research that may be best done by beginning before you start writing your plan. You may need a few trips to the library for census data or to find your SIC code or even to get the help of a good reference librarian. You might want to hire a consultant or research firm. It's all a matter of how much time and/or money you have to spare. Market research takes time and you must plan for that time if you are going to meet your goals and timelines.

The "how's" and "what's" of your market research should be included in The Marketing section. Discuss how you did the research and what you found out. What resources did you use? Your resources and your methods should back up your numbers and add an element of expertise. Did you use Census data or questionnaires? Did you test your results? Did you talk to experts in the field? Did you hire outside sources to do all or part of your marketing research? If so, why did you choose that source? Even if you did contract the work out, your plan should display your understanding of the results.

What were the results of your market research? What did you find out about your target market(s)? What is the status of markets -- are they growing, steady or declining? The same is true for market share. How do you see your share changing over time? Is the market big enough for you to move in and is it big enough for you to grow in?

You should include a list or discussion of the demographics of target markets, but don't be afraid to get specific. The specifics are what will set your business plan apart. For example, maybe your research shows you that members of your target market will only frequent stores within a five-mile radius of their homes. If your research bears this out and you have planned your office supply store in a remote area zoned for only industrial uses, any potential investor or partner is going to see a major flaw in your plan. Ideally, you will see this major flaw as well and change your plans accordingly. Another example: say your demographic information shows there are only 11 home-owned copiers in your town. You might not want to stack 50 home-copiers in your office supply store and you won't likely want to offer home-copier repair as a service (unless someone on your staff can do that as well as other duties). However, if your business is in a rural area with a lot of virtual commuters, in-home copier repair may be a viable service niche for you to enter so long as you can make it cost-effective.

With all your great research in hand and in mind, discuss how your particular business strengths, resources and experience can serve your target market(s). Be realistic. Passion is great; enthusiasm is absolutely necessary for business start up. Try to reign in your enthusiasm when writing your marketing section. No matter how nifty-keen your product or service is to you, it is not going to appeal to or be of use to everyone. Show that you know this in your business plan. The minute you start saying that your stapler will revolutionize office work as we know it and that no office will be able to compete without it, you will lose your audience. If your stapler is that magnificent, show that fact through numbers. Back up your statements, assumptions and projections with data. Keep in mind the amount of time and effort (let alone resources and cost) it will take to serve a target market and be sure your goals are attainable. Leave the pie in the sky to the birds.

If you are writing your plan for a franchise, include the strategy developed by the franchisor, including what help the franchisor offers to franchise owners. With the strategy in hand, how will you increase sales?

If you are writing your plan for an existing business, discuss who your existing customers are. Review how you have attracted customers. How will you retain the customers you have and how will you promote your product to new customers? Marketing is about expanding your market. Address the issue clearly.

Competition

Tony

Tony was struggling with his business plan. He wanted to open a small, service-oriented bicycle shop and needed to raise $75,000 to get started. But drafting the plan was a huge roadblock for him. The words did not come easily. Still, Tony knew he had to see it through -- not only to attract the start up monies from friends and family, but also to focus his thinking and create a game plan for moving forward.

But Tony had no experience writing a business plan. He had graduated from Berkeley with a degree in people's liberation studies. His college courses left him thoroughly unprepared to write seriously about business issues. And the bare bones template he was working from said he needed to discuss certain issues, but gave no hints or insights on how to do so.

Tony was particularly stuck on the section labeled "Competition." What was he supposed to write? His Berkeley professors would have him put forth: "We live in a fascist/capitalist system dominated by powerful, oligarchical multinational corporations which tolerate limited competition for the shrinking sector of economic activity they do not yet control."

Whether true or not, how inspiring was that? Tony instinctively knew that people didn't invest in a downer. He knew that just as having positive energy could be contagious and transformational, negative energy could suck the life out of people. So, how could you write about competition in a happy, positive 'Here's-my-money-I-want-to-invest' kind of way? Wasn't competition a downer that kept people from even considering investing your business?

Fortunately, Tony's old roommate at Cal had studied in the business department. Tony invited Jamal to lunch to pick his brain about how to deal with the competition conundrum.

Jamal's first advice for Tony was that he had to stop thinking about competition in the ominous Marxist/world domination terms presented by his professors. For business guys, competition brought innovation, efficiency and greater employment. Competition brought choices and freedom. Competition was fun. Jamal noted that competition was one of the first sections competitive business guys read. It got their juices flowing just to read how you were going to beat the pants off your competition. Bigger, better, smarter: How was Tony going to stick it to the other guys?

Tony nodded as Jamal became even more animated in explaining the importance of the competition section of a business plan. He compared it to a novel or a movie, both of which needed conflict and dramatic tension to succeed. Without conflict or competition, what do you have? How many people sat through a film about people exploring their inner feelings to no end? You only needed to see one French government funded film to know you'd never pay to see another. Jamal then laughed and said that such terminally boring movies were only made in the absence of competition. They would never get made in America's highly competitive movie industry because they lacked the necessary ingredient of conflict.

So just as great literature featured conflict so should a great business plan. And conflict was found in the competition section of the plan. Competition was a challenge for the entrepreneur/hero to overcome. You didn't slink away from it. You met it head on with the knowledge and determination to prevail.

Tony was energized by the new approach Jamal presented. But how would it work for his plan?

Jamal said Tony's plan was easy. First, he needed to do some research. There was plenty of information on the Internet. He could access news stories of how small independent bicycle shops across America held their own against the large sporting goods stores. What were their strategies? Tony could learn from their experiences. He could call a few of these dealers up and ask for advice on his plan. Most people were happy to help someone new to the business get started. He could also get information on public companies in the industry at www.sec.gov. Each one of those public reports, known as 10Ks and 10Qs, had discussions on competition. It was all at his fingertips.

Once Tony's research was complete the writing would be easy. Jamal saw that Tony's competitive advantage would be in product knowledge and service. While the large national sporting goods chains could offer lower prices they couldn't match the personal service of a local shop. And Jamal knew that a certain percentage of the population was willing to pay extra for that service. Tony needed to do the research to see if that percentage was quantified. If the exact number wasn't available, so be it. Identifying the conflict between large and small was enough. The battle was joined, the enemy identified and the competition begun.

Tony paid for lunch and thanked Jamal for his insights. As Jamal departed he reminded Tony to have fun with competition.

No matter how great your business idea, no matter how thorough your description of your business and financing, you have to address competition in your plan. Again, think in terms of who, what, where and how.

Who is your competition? Are their sales going up or down? Is the competition direct (offering the same product or service to the same customer base) or indirect (offering the same product or service but to a different target market) or both? How is the competition targeting the market? How can you target the market better? Are there untapped markets you can target? What are your different strategies for both direct and indirect competitors?

In order to answer any of these questions, you will need an in-depth understanding of industry norms and trends, your business strengths and weaknesses and the strengths, weaknesses, operations and perceptions of your competition. Research is your friend.

At a minimum, you will want to know the names and locations of major competitors, products or services offered, pricing structure, methods of distribution, strengths, weaknesses, profitability and market share. In addition, you will be served by an analysis of how the competition is viewed by current or potential customers. What is the reputation of your competition? Review how each competitor built its reputation, be it through promotion, packaging, price, quality, and/or advertising. Consider the experience of your major competitors and what their missions, goals and objectives are. How has the competition performed in the past and how is each competitor positioned for the future? Be sure to analyze all your major competitors separately. Beware of cutting corners and making assumptions. Take a little time here and you will not only improve your business plan, but you'll also improve your business.

There are many ways to find out about your competition. The Internet is replete with information. Again, an excellent way to find out about public companies is through annual and quarterly reports at www.sec.gov. Other good sources include stock market reports and just talking to customers, suppliers and distributors.

Don't forget about tomorrow. Where will future competitors come from? Can you foresee any expansions of existing firms? Do you see any firms gearing up to make new products or offer new services that would compete with your product or service? Can any of your customers duplicate your product or service in-house? Are any of your competitors pursuing intellectual property rights that could affect your business?

With your analysis in mind, how can you use the information you have gathered to improve your market share? Can you use your strengths to capture customers through marketing or advertising? Can you use the strengths of your competition to improve your operations? Can you use your competition's weaknesses to narrow your target market or improve your product or service?

If you are writing your plan for an existing business, address how you have dealt with competition in the past and how you will change your approach in the future. What is your timeline for your marketing plan?

If you are writing your business plan for a new business, address how you will enter the market and when. Be sure to address how your knowledge of the competition will color your plans.

Don't let your knowledge of the competition begin and end with your business plan. Keep an eye on the competition at all times. Learn from their mistakes and their successes. Keep up on the operational and advertising efforts of the competition and watch how and when strategies change. Then try to figure out why.

Distribution and Sales

By now, you should have a good handle on your business and on the competition. But you can't make a sale unless you can physically deliver your product or service to the customer. That's where distribution comes in. Distribution should be a result of your marketing research. For example, you don't want to set up your entire system to deliver products through catalog sales only to find out that your target market only buys in-store. Be sure you understand the purchasing patterns of your target customers and then set up your business to make use of those patterns.

Give an overview of your distribution strategy, including any and all channels available to you. What relationships currently exist? What changes do you see in the future? How will you deal with increased or decreased distribution needs?

Be sure to include a discussion of any shipping necessary to your business. Review what shipping resources you will use and why. What will this cost you, what backup plans do you have and what agreements do you have with distributors? Include agreement documents, rates and any other supporting documents that might back up your plans.

If your plan is for a service business, include a discussion of how you will handle delivering services. Will you go to customers or will they come to you, and who will pay for travel? How quickly do you anticipate being able to meet customer service needs?

As for sales, will you be selling business to business or directly to customers? Who will be doing the selling? Will you have a sales department, sales staff, consultants or a mixture? Describe how many sales people you will have of each kind for each service or product. Give a brief summary, but don't worry about the details. How will sales be conducted -- in-store, online, catalog, direct mail, retail, etc.? If you use direct mail, where will you get your mailing lists? If you use the Internet, what is your Web strategy? If you use retail, what stores will you have a presence in? What discounts will you offer, to whom and under what circumstances? If sales decrease or increase significantly, how will you handle it? As we have mentioned before, not all of these questions may apply to your exact situation. But you need to address the ones that are on point in order to come up with a winning business plan.

In many cases, you will prepare a forecast of future sales. A detailed sales forecast should include a month-by-month spreadsheet of shipments and sales prices for each product or service. If prices or the volume are expected to change, this should be explained. If customer classes are expected to change, explain that as well. Anything that affects your revenue projection should be detailed here. Give your data in several ways, such as by product, by region and by target market, so that the data can be more easily understood. Be sure to note how you arrived at your numbers, whether it was through market research, expert opinions, staff experience or the like. If you are writing your plan for an existing business, you can use past revenue numbers to further back up your forecast. If you are writing the plan for a franchise, get existing data from the franchisor and describe how your business will meet franchise expectations by using existing distribution channels and relationships.

If you are writing a business plan for a new business, you will need to use a good bit of extrapolation to add some hard data to this section. But if you are writing your plan for an existing business, include real numbers and names. Go ahead and add some detail as to who you use as distributors along with their revenues, production, market share or whatever data might help you sell your idea or manage your business.

Rich Dad Tips

- Many entrepreneurs do not like to include a detailed sale forecast in their business plan. The thought is that too many investors will hold you to those speculative numbers.

- Even if you do not include one, consider preparing it ahead of time. Some investors will want to see a sales forecast before investing. You are better off having it ready than scrambling to assemble it later.

Getting The Word Out

There's always a chance that a customer could trip over a crack in the sidewalk and fall right into your shop. But the odds are that there will never be enough customers finding you without any sort of marketing to keep you in business. Advertising, public relations, promotions -- they are all about the same thing: getting your product or service before potential customers. A sign on your shop is marketing. Your spouse telling a friend is marketing. Your business card and stationary and even your business plan are marketing. Just about everything you do or say can be construed as marketing. But ideally your marketing plan will be more focused than this.

Though it might be tempting to lump any and all marketing endeavors together, consider breaking this subsection into further subsections to prove your knowledge in this area. For example, any paid marketing endeavors (advertisements) come under the subheading "Advertising." Here you can address your ad campaign plans -- by location (local, regional or national), media (television, radio, newspaper, Internet, and the like) and audience (trade or consumers). Promotions are those endeavors designed to increase sales but that don't usually involve paying for image. Think sales, coupons and the like. Public relations ("PR") are the indirect efforts that bring notoriety to your company, products or services. Say you sponsor a charity event and your name is mentioned in that charity's advertising, that's PR. Social Media is now an important marketing channel for both large and small businesses. Be sure to include a statement on how you will address this forum. You might also want to include subsections on trade shows, direct mail, Internet and catalog. As always, include only those sections and subsections pertinent to your business and include detail judiciously.

We come back to the market research you did. The results of your research should help you determine the best advertising campaign for your product or service. Keep those target markets fresh in your brain. Are your potential customers reached more efficiently by radio or television? Which stations do your target customers listen to and when? Do they read newspapers or magazines or find all of their information online? If so, which ones and how often?

Go back to your research on the competition. Where do competitors advertise? How and how often? Do competitor ad campaigns work? Why or why not? Learn from the successes and failures, strengths and weaknesses, of the competition. Learn, copy, improve. Let your readers know that you will test your advertising to see what medium is most effective.

Explain your advertising plan in this subsection and include any visuals you have (brochures, print ads, mail pieces, etc.). Who will be handling your marketing campaign -- staff, consultants, or an outside firm? How much will it cost to implement your plan? Break down the costs of your advertising plan so potential investors and partners can see how their money will be spent. Give a timeline for your campaign -- when will which ads drop, when will mail pieces go out, when will radio or TV ads play? As always, explain your decision-making process (and show off all your marketing knowledge).

Of course, if you are writing your plan for an existing business, you should summarize your past marketing attempts. Discuss whether or not they worked and why or why not. Give an analysis of what was spent and what was gained from the marketing expenditures, including what you learned from past experiences.

If you are writing your plan for a franchise, keep in mind that the franchisors have likely come up with advertising materials and plans already. And odds are that they know what they are doing (after all, they've built a product or service into a franchise). Some franchisors will not allow you to use materials or plans you develop independently. Others may approve such materials or plans if they are deemed appropriate. But even if there are no rules on using independently derived materials, you should make sure your plans coincide with or compliment those of the franchiser. And you should let franchisors in on your plans, which is probably required by the franchise agreement anyway.

Franchisors can help by offering advice and alternatives. They've likely been at this longer than you, have better research and resources and may have a multipart plan that precludes your ideas. On the other hand, your ideas may be just the breath of fresh air franchisors have been looking for. It's your call -- go with what is provided, work with your own ideas in concert with the franchisors or come up with something completely new. Just know the expectations of those with whom you will be working. And again, know what you agreed to in the franchise agreement.

Whatever you do in business, know that marketing is a key component of your success. Products and services rarely sell in a vacuum. Your marketing plan must be focused and thoughtful. Investors who see a well-written plan for marketing will think in terms of a winning business plan.

Chapter Eleven

Marketing Trends and Timing

"Trends are your friends."
– Anonymous

Sam

Sam was preparing a business plan for a real estate investment he wanted to make. He knew that he would have to persuasively present exactly how his project would deliver superior cash flow so that the bank would extend him financing.

Sam was interested in a 40-unit apartment complex in an older part of town. He prepared his plan using all of the real estate business plan template headings. He thoroughly analyzed all of the rents in the market and was familiar with all of the comparables. After his review he knew he could raise rents by 10% in six months without a problem.

Sam had his maintenance experts review the property to see what repairs needed to be made. He did not like to deal with deferred maintenance when he owned a property. Sam's strategy was to only deal with properties there were structurally and cosmetically sound, and charge rents accordingly for the suitable product. Of course, buying a property with deferred maintenance was a different issue. Sam aggressively used a lack of repairs to obtain a reduced selling price from the buyer.

But it was Sam's strategy of buying somewhat distressed properties in older parts of towns that had caused him troubles with various bankers. The current conventional wisdom was that you couldn't make money on such properties. The reasons were legion: Interest rates were headed up. There were new apartments being built in newer, nicer parts of town. The market for homes was competing with apartments. And conventional wisdom was very much the banker's currency. Sam knew that bankers wouldn't (and really couldn't) trade in the untested, unsound and uncertain. Instead, conventional wisdom was a comfortable place for banks to operate from.

For this reason Sam had learned to be very aware of market trends and timing. If the conventional wisdom of the day about the market and market factors was X, Sam knew he had to argue to X, or overcome X.

In the case of the 40-unit apartment complex he was now looking to acquire, Sam had already heard from one banker that the town was growing away from the downtown core. The conventional wisdom was that the complex was in a decaying and depreciating part of town. Sam knew he had to overcome this impression.

Fortunately, Sam was in a well-connected lead group. In communities all across America, there are groups that meet once or twice a month for breakfast or lunch to share leads and market intelligence on what is happening around town. Sam had been in such a local group for ten years and had learned of inside information and developments weeks and sometimes months before the news became public.

At this last meeting Sam had learned some interesting information about the old county hospital, which happened to be just three blocks away from the apartment building he wanted to purchase. It wasn't public yet but it would soon be announced that the hospital was going to build a $100 million ten-story medical office building. Over 300 new jobs would be opening up in the neighborhood.

Sam called the banker to see if he had heard of this news. The banker was surprised and said he needed to quickly make some calls. An hour later he called Sam back to thank him from the tip. He also suggested Sam send over the business plan for the 40-unit complex. There was new interest in lending for acquisitions in the neighborhood.

Whether for real estate or any other business, knowing your market and the trends within it are crucial for your business plan.

Your business exists within a series of ever-expanding spheres of influence. The discussion of these spheres as elements affecting your business will be the bulk of the Industry and Market Trends subsection of your plan. Be sure you understand each factor and how it influences your business.

Some of these elements may have little or no bearing on your business. That's fine, but you may want to address that lack of influence in your business plan as well. The elements to consider include:

- your business
- the competition
- the market
- the industry
- the government
- international affairs
- other market factors

In the center of all these spheres of influence is your business. (You knew it was the center of the universe, right?) You have discussed your business thoroughly in previous sections and subsections of your plan, so you don't need to go into a description again here. In this subsection, readers are more concerned with how your business interacts with the other elements or outside forces and how those interactions currently and will affect your business' potential for making money. So discuss how your business is affected by the competition, the market, and the industry you are in.

Consider how competitive the industry is and how easy it has been for new ventures to break in? How healthy, financially, is the industry? What are average profit margins within the industry? Are costs rising or falling in your industry? How powerful are distributors, customers and suppliers when it comes to setting industry price norms? Does your industry go through cycles? What does the future hold in terms of trends within the industry? How did past trends affect the industry? How does technology affect the industry and how will new discoveries influence the future? How often does technology shape industry norms?

The sphere of government influences your business, the competition, the market and the industry. Regulatory changes, interest rates, even government contracts are constantly constricting and loosening, changing the shape and density of the other spheres. What regulatory bodies have influence on your industry? What regulations apply? Do you have intellectual property rights that may lose protection through expiration? What do you foresee happening in the realm of governmental influences that could impact your business, be it negatively or positively?

It doesn't end there. United States governmental influences are affected by international relationships. How does the relative strength or weakness of the dollar affect your company? Are there geographic areas whose instability threatens your industry? Is war in the offing? What is the state of the world economy, and does that affect your company?

There may be even more questions that affect your particular plan. Weather is an issue if you sell suntan oil or snow tires. It is an issue if you operate in a tornado belt.

All these spheres of influence are in a near-constant state of flux. But being aware of them and their potential changes can put you ahead of the crowd.

Pricing Strategy

Don't leave any aspect of your business to chance. The whole idea behind writing your business plan is to plan your business strategy. Whether you are preparing your plan for management or funding purposes, you want to work out all the kinks you can before you ever set up shop. Do your planning and experimentation on paper whenever possible. Get your plan in the best shape you can before you use it. But once you do start to show it around, don't be afraid of change. Remain flexible. Thoughts are free. Paper is cheap. Real-life business mistakes are costly.

Just as your distribution plan should come after your market research, pricing should be based on a careful analysis of production costs and overhead, competition and target markets. Pricing may be part of your marketing plan or it may be a stand-alone subsection in your business plan. As with every other section of your business plan, put Pricing where it makes the most sense.

Pricing is closely tied into costs and market dynamics. First, you need to know how much it costs you to deliver your products and/or services to customers. Be sure to take all costs into account -- from raw materials to shipping costs, from office rents or leases to taxes, from payroll to advertising, from lawyer fees to construction. Make sure your pricing will cover not only day-to-day operating costs, but contingency plans as well. Address how pricing may change over time based on market changes and cost changes over time. Is there a floodgate sales number that will allow you to purchase supplies at a discount or bulk rate? Will your pricing reflect such a change in costs? If so, why? If not, why not?

Once you have a handle on your costs, you need to understand your competition's pricing, customer perceptions and market norms. How much does the competition charge for the same or similar products or services? How did your competitors arrive at their pricing strategies? How do customers perceive the value of the product or service (what is your product or service worth)? What is the real and perceived quality of your product or service? What are considered the high and low-end prices for similar (or the same) products or services? Will your pricing plan come in at the high end or the low end? Be prepared to explain your price -- why you chose it, and how it will benefit profits and/or business longevity.

Services may be harder to price. Again, you need to understand the value of your offering to your business as well as the perceived value to your customers. Consultants don't just charge for the cost of paper and ink even if the only tangible product is a report. Clearly, what the consultant offers is more valuable than simply the tangible. Service offerings solve problems, offer expertise, save time, and/or save clients from doing things they'd rather not do. Still, pricing needs to reflect market norms.

Obviously you don't want to set your prices too much higher than your competition even if your expertise or experience might warrant it. If your price outweighs the perceived value of the service, you won't attract customers. However, if your price is too much lower than that of the competition, you run the risk of lowering the perceived value of your service and again losing customers.

Many a business has been a success based on the old cliché of "you get what you pay for." There will always be a segment of the market willing to pay for nothing more than prestige.

Rich Dad Tips

- Pricing is both a science and an art. While numbers and calculations will lead to a possible price, remember to leverage innovative marketing to command a higher price.

- Most entrepreneurs underestimate costs when starting out a business. Before pricing is set, make sure you understand all of your costs and build a cushion to prepare for the inevitable unexpected costs that occur.

- Know where you want your price to be within your market. While the luxury end of the market can be difficult, the margins can be significant. The ability to serve more people comes from serving the masses with everyday goods.

Keep in mind that your pricing plan should include more than just a sticker price. Do you or will you offer discounts? If so, how much (a range is fine; you don't need detail) and under what conditions? What are the terms under which discounts will be granted or offered? How about your return policy? Under what conditions do you or will you allow returns? How are returns handled (on-site, return mail, company pickup)? Will customers be eligible for cash back, replacement products or services or credit? Is there a time limit on returns? Do you offer a product or service warranty? If so, what are the terms?

Beware of basing your entire business on the idea of undercutting the prices of the competition. While low prices may bring customers in, it doesn't take much for the competition to catch on and match those low prices. Then what? You lower your prices again? The cycle quickly sucks down weak businesses. Be sure that you have more to offer than a low price -- something that gives you a true edge over the competition, an edge the competition can't duplicate.

Once you have set a pricing plan, explain your reasoning. As always, back up your plan with statistics and research wherever you can.

If you are writing your plan for a franchise, you may think you don't need to worry about pricing. After all, price is usually set by the franchisor. But price will still and always affect your profits. Be sure you understand your franchise and the larger industry well enough to recognize when industry trends and pricing could start eating away at profits.

Timing

Part of your business strategy should be the timing of your entry into the market. You might think that there's no strategy involved. You enter the market as soon as you start the business, right? Not necessarily. Your market entry should be more about the customer than it is about you. So try to put aside your eagerness and do a little research to see if your customers are ready for your business. Would your customers be more likely to buy your product or service during winter or summer? Will weather affect sales? Can you tie in your business opening with a holiday or special event? Is there a regulatory or technological change in the offing that might help increase your market share? Check existing data on consumer spending patterns. For example, data shows that consumers are more likely to purchase from catalogs in September than in July.

Use common sense. Don't introduce your line of beach umbrellas to Denver in December. Knowing when consumers buy what products or services when can help you infuse your business with a quick influx of sales during the crucial startup time, giving you a better chance of early profits (and thus a quicker return on investment for partners, bankers and the like).

Of course, it may be hard (or even impossible) to wait for the ideal launch time. You may choose to startup sales of products or services on a small scale for a time. Quietly beginning business can allow you time to work out the kinks in your operation before things get too hectic. Then once you have everything running smoothly, you can launch your advertising campaign and have a grand opening celebration. If you know your business and your market, you should have a fairly good idea as to whether it is better for you to blitz or wait. Either way, make compelling arguments as to the choices in your business plan.

Product Design and Packaging

Consumers today are bombarded with products and services. You want as many consumers as possible to ignore the barrage and see your product or service for the superior, innovative, valuable problem-solver it is. Some consumers will come to their buying decisions through the internet or advertising, others through word of mouth, some through experience, but many will make their decision based on packaging design. The physical appearance of your product (or the way you present your service) is your first chance to make an impression on consumers. What do you want that impression to be? More importantly, what impression will help convince consumers to part with their hard-earned cash?

Get to know the taste and preference of your target market as well as some of the psychology behind packaging. What are your competitors using? Is it working? Don't skip the research. You never get a second chance to make a first impression -- cliché, but true. But another important factor to remember is that your first impression may haunt you longer than you would ever guess. Every time you change your design -- be it a logo or a box -- you start your branding all over again. Visual recognition (or auditory in the case of jingles) is strong. Sometimes changing your product packaging design can cause more confusion than changing your product name. Get it right the first time and watch your business build on its own momentum.

A note of caution: Some products have mandatory labeling requirements. Find out what information you might have to include on your product and incorporate it in even your most preliminary design discussions.

When you think packaging you might just think products only. But even services use packaging design. If you offer copier repair, what does your contract look like? How about your list of services? Copier repair can be high tech. If you hand your client a faded, poorly reproduced, crumpled piece of paper as a statement of qualifications, does this really give the image you think will help you land the contract?

Explain your decisions in your business plan and back up those decisions with your research and your findings about your customers' tastes and preferences. Include visuals wherever you can -- label designs, photos of box mockups, introductory service materials -- whatever applies to your particular business.

Positioning

Positioning is simply a way to separate your product or service from that of the competition. Explain how your product or service is unique and/or how it will take unique advantage of the potential market. In other words, explain how you will convince customers to buy your product or service.

First you need to address what the difference is, be it price, distribution, features, quality, and/or variety. Then you need to address how you will bring that difference to the attention of potential customers. This need not be a complicated subsection, but it does require a very thorough understanding of your business and the market in which your business exists. The positioning section is the culmination of all of your market, competition and industry trends research. It is where you stand.

By supplementing your Marketing section with the right addition of market trends and timing information you will go a long way towards creating the winning business plan.

Chapter Twelve

Funding and Financials

"Money never starts an idea; it is the idea that starts the money."
– William J. Cameron

Gina

Gina had a fledgling coffee and cookie business. She had three kiosks at the three largest malls selling cookies, coffees and chocolate snacks.

Gina's Java, Inc. had been open for two and a half years. Gina had managed to fund the start up phase of $50,000 with her own personal funds. This allowed her to open the first location. She had prudently formed a corporation and immediately started to build her corporate credit. She also hired a bookkeeping firm to keep track of her financial activities from the start. After six months of success at kiosk number one, Gina was able to use other money to expand the business. The fact that Gina had quickly built up her corporate credit and had accurate financials ready to show was important to the banker. Her first bank line of credit was extended to the business but required a personal guarantee. If the business failed to make a payment to the bank then Gina would be personally responsible for the payment. This was alright with Gina. She knew that if she failed to provide a personal guarantee at the start, she would never get to the point where a personal guarantee wasn't required. She knew she had to build up the business using her own personal credit at the start.

Gina's second credit line was used to expand into the third kiosk location. Because business had performed so well, and because Gina had done such a good job of promptly establishing corporate credit, she did not have to provide a personal guarantee for the second line of credit. The bank looked only to the ability of Gina's Java Inc. to repay the loan, and not to Gina as a backup guarantor. As Gina's banker had put it, any business that can get over and over again $3 for a cup of colored water is liquid enough to repay a small loan.

Month after month Gina paid her bills on time. Month after month her corporate credit grew stronger and stronger.

Gina was soon presented with a very interesting offer. A new downtown dining center was being opened. Only four vendors were being allowed into a high traffic location in the heart of the city. Gina was intrigued and felt that Gina's Java would do quite well in the area, despite the presence of Starbucks a block away. But she was also concerned by the $350,000 cost to participate. She knew her bankers would not extend that much credit either to her business or to her personally to get the new location opened.

Gina spoke to her attorney and CPA about how to proceed. The more she investigated the downtown dining center, the better she felt about doing the deal.

Gina's lawyer advised her on a number of issues, but one item really stood out. It was something Gina had never considered before. It had to do with how to raise the $350,000 needed. Gina had always assumed that she would have to give up a percentage of her ownership in Gina's Java Inc. This didn't really appeal to her since she had used her own money and sweat equity to build up a now profitable business. She wasn't too keen on giving that away.

And so Gina's lawyer suggested an alternative. Gina could form a new corporation just to operate the downtown location. In this way Gina wouldn't have to give away any ownership in the three kiosks she had worked so hard to build up. At the same time, the investors coming in would get a higher percentage of ownership in the new entity, Gina's Downtown Java Inc., since their money would be material to the success of the new business. Gina liked this idea.

Gina's lawyer and CPA both pointed out that the current and projected financials would be crucial for the plan to succeed. Investors would want to see the current and up to date financial history for the kiosks. This information and track record would help them to analyze Gina's projections for the new downtown location.

The CPA also cautioned that the projections for the new location should not be too optimistic. The fact that Gina's kiosks had done well right from the start should not be built into the downtown projections. Investors shied away from overly optimistic too-good-to-be-true projections, even if Gina believed them to be true. The CPA noted that it was better to have the investors pleasantly surprised by a better-than-expected performance than complaining that unreasonably high projections were not met.

With this pathway clearly understood, Gina prepared her business plan. Her bookkeeper had kept good records from the start and they were able to pull together the following reports for Gina's Java Inc.:

- Income Statement
- Balance Sheet
- Cash Flow Statement

They then used this information to prepare the following projections for Gina's Downtown Java Inc.:

- Income Projection
- Break-Even Analysis
- Use of Funds

The investors liked having the track record of an existing business to compare with the projections for the new business. They felt that Gina's proposal was fair given her record and understanding of the market

The plan for Gina's Downtown Java was funded. The investors were pleasantly surprised by a better-than-expected performance.

Whether you are preparing your plan for an existing business or a startup, whether you are preparing a plan to attract funding or to guide management, you need to address financials. There are no free rides. The next two chapters explain how you will go about paying for everything you described in the rest of the plan and (often more importantly) how you will make a profit doing so. Whereas the other sections have room for persuasion through your words, the financials need to sell the business by the numbers. Funding and Financials go hand in hand. The Financials tell you have much you need for Funding and the Funding relates back to how much profit there is in the Financials.

Rich Dad Tips

- Because writing The Business and The Marketing sections are the real planning sections of the business plan, write them first. It is through the writing of these sections that you will clarify your own goals, mission and plans.

- Do not write The Financials section first or you will most likely end up having to redo it after you write the others.

Your numbers in The Financials section need to reflect the text in the other sections. In many ways, your text in The Business and The Marketing sections will provide the assumptions of your Financials section. (This does not mean you don't need the Assumptions subsection, however. Never make your readers guess. Spell out the reasoning for your numbers in the Assumptions subsection even if you think that reasoning is perfectly clear in your Business and Marketing sections.)

As you write The Business and The Marketing sections, keep notes on how each of your decisions and plans will affect the money side of the business. For example, you've decided how many employees you need, but how much will personnel cost you when you add in benefits, overtime and worker's compensation? How much will it cost to transport products and materials from and to your proposed location? How much will your advertising campaign cost and how much can you realistically expect it to bring in? How will industry norms and trends affect your pricing and how will that pricing change your profitability over time?

Obviously, if you are writing a plan for an existing business, some of your financial information will come from actual spending and revenues. Or as in Gina's case, you can use a previous financial history to assist with future projections. In both cases this is certainly easier than trying to extrapolate. However, if you are writing your plan for a new business venture, you really have no choice but to extrapolate. Yet, that extrapolation will still be based on real data. Any number you put into your business plan needs to be backed up by research and/or expertise. And that research and/or expertise needs to be highlighted within the plan.

Guessing can kill a plan. The people charged with making financial and investment decisions based on your plan likely know a lot more about financials than you do. After all, they have likely seen a lot more business plans than you have and are experienced at weighing the potential risks and rewards involved with backing a business endeavor. Don't try to snow the experts. They know the difference between snowflakes and flakes.

It is tempting to try to fudge the numbers a bit here and there, tweaking them to make your case. Don't. The minute any of your numbers is called into question, your whole plan is called into question. Remember financial readers are trying to decide whether or not they can trust your business to return their money. If they can't trust your figures, they can't trust you. Possibly even worse, if your management staff sees errors in your numbers (or just unrealistic assumptions), then they will doubt your knowledge of the business. Neither situation helps your business.

This section is the meat-and-potatoes section of the business plan written to attract investment. We've talked about which sections of the plan get read first by whom. For numbers guys Financials are the first sections read. But don't put the Financials up front. By putting it near the end, you increase the chance of readers looking through the whole plan. You want them to understand the concept, not just the numbers involved. Some plan preparers include The Financials section as a stand-alone document so that they might control when and under what circumstances readers see the information. That strategy may make sense in some cases. Do what suits your business best.

Keep in mind that the numbers you put into your financial spreadsheets are not the point of The Financials section. Rather, the numbers are merely symbols standing in for principles. It is the principles that you need to understand. Many first-time business owners are at their shakiest when dealing with numbers. They often have no background whatsoever in accounting practices and principles. If you fall into this category, don't let your lack of familiarity with numbers sink your plan. You can always hire someone to do the numbers based on your input and the text from the other sections. But don't go walking into an interview with a potential lender or investor without having a thorough understanding of what those numbers mean.

What You Need and Why

As with the other sections, the opening of your Financials section should be a one-page overview of the financial data. The rest of the section will be little more than expansion on that overview.

If you are preparing your plan for the purposes of attracting funding, you will need to know how much to ask for and what you are willing to give in return -- interest, ownership and the like. Through your research and writing of The Business and The Marketing sections, you should have a good idea of how much money you will need.

Whether you are looking for funding for a startup business, an expansion of your existing business, franchise purchase, purchase of a traditional business, promotional activities or an introduction of a new product or service, you will need money. If you don't have all the cash you need, you will need to seek outside funding through investments, loans or a combination of the two. In most cases, you will need cash on hand to pay for any (or all) costs that lead you to your break-even date (when revenues equal costs), which may very well be years in the offing. These costs will include everything from payroll to advertising, insurance to office supplies, security to equipment, buildings to vehicles, research to raw materials. You might even want to allow a salary for yourself. The key is to be sure you know every single cost facing your business and know that you have adequately estimated the size of those costs.

What financial information should you include in your plan? It depends. Different financial institutions and individuals have different preferences as to what they want to see. The needs of a management team differ from those of financial backers, and the needs of bank personnel are different from those of venture capitalists.

While you may not be able to structure one plan to fit all readers, you can prepare the standards and then tailor your plan for individual uses. You don't want to overwhelm readers with too much information or information that won't impact their decision-making process. You risk losing pertinent information in a wash of numbers. You also don't want to risk giving unneeded information that might actually hurt your chances of getting funding. (Know when to quit and never talk past the sale). Nor do you want to give away information that would be better off left between you and your managers.

In general, most plans include information about:
- how much money is needed to operate the business (income statement, cash flow statement, balance sheet, income projection)
- how borrowed funds will be used (use of funds)
- how much and how company funds will be used (income statement, cash flow statement, balance sheet, income projection)
- how much money is needed in the future (income projection)
- the break-even point (break-even analysis)
- current and past spending (income statement, cash flow statement, balance sheet)

You will be looking at business forecasts (or projections) and/or business statements. Forecasts are goals, statements are how well you meet those goals.

For purposes of existing businesses, include at a minimum:
Uses of Funds
Cash Flow Statement
Income Statement
Income Projection
Break-Even Analysis
Balance Sheet
Business Financial History or Loan Application (if applicable)

For a new business, you will have no business history, so you need only include:
Uses of Funds
Cash Flow Statement
Income Projection
Break-Even Analysis
Loan Application (if applicable)

Because starting up a new business involves a lot of one-time costs, it is also helpful to include a startup budget. This way you can get an accurate picture of what you will need to get your business up and running, but you will also be able to separate these costs (to a degree) from other costs. A startup budget should include expenses such as utility deposits, major equipment, down payments, legal and professional fees, permits and licenses and contractor services.

After you have prepared all your financial documents, you might want to consider yet one more document -- this one for your own personal use – a funding plan. A funding plan is exactly what it sounds like -- a plan for how you will achieve adequate money to fund your business. Your plan should include how many rounds of funding you will implement, when you will begin each round, how long each round will ideally last, how much money you will ask for in each round, what the funds will be used for and from whom you will seek the money in each round.

No matter how thorough and accurate your numbers may be, decision-makers always have the option of not paying a bit of attention to them. They may take some of your numbers as a basis for their own analysis (after all, odds are they've got quite a good idea of what it will take to run a business as laid out in your plan) or they may discount the whole lot. Part of this will depend on the perceived accuracy of your numbers and how realistic the decision-makers think you are in your projections and extrapolations, but part of it will simply depend on the experience of those making the decisions.

Types of Funding

There are many ways to finance a business, and entrepreneurs are known for their creativity in this arena. Most financing falls into two broad categories: equity financing and non-equity financing. Equity financing is where you give up partial ownership of your business in exchange for funding. Non-equity financing is where you agree to pay back funding provided to you from others (usually plus interest). Financing may also incorporate a combination of the two.

Where you get financing is a matter of how much you need and what you are willing to exchange. The following is a brief summary of common sources of business funding:

Non-equity Funding

Entities that offer loans only are looking to be paid back -- that's it. Their interest in the business is that you will make enough to make good on the loan. Their financial interest is in the interest. These entities (such as banks) are not particularly concerned with the long-term health of your business if that long term exceeds the life of the loan. Nor do they particularly care how much your business grows so long as it grows enough to enable you to keep making those payments on time.

Banks

You think of loans, you think of banks. Even with the other options open to today's entrepreneur, banks are still the most common place from which to borrow money. But don't go thinking that you can just walk in, fill out a loan application and walk out with a bag of cash. Banks are institutions, yes, but those institutions are made up of people and people are more likely to help out people they know. So let the bank get to know you. Choose a bank where you are comfortable doing business, a bank that knows business people like you and has a track record of taking a risk on your kind of business. Choose your banker carefully because he or she can be a valuable ally in foraying into the often confusing world of financing a business.

Your Funds

There's very little chance of you going into business without using personal assets. If you can swing it and you don't want to be beholden, personal assets are about the best way to fund a business. This can mean breaking open your piggy bank, converting investments into cash and tapping bank accounts. But you'll still want to start building a separate business credit profile. For more information on such strategies visit www.businesscreditsuccess.com.

Even if you can't completely fund the business through your assets, plan on using them anyway. Potential investors like to know you are putting your own finances on the line before you ask them to do the same. They like to see that you are serious enough to risk your own money.

Credit Unions

Credit unions operate a lot like banks but are only open to members. Government agencies, labor unions and some companies offer credit union membership to their people. Check to see if you belong to a group that offers such membership.

Loan and Finance Companies

These companies are in the business of loaning people money for business use, be it to purchase equipment, use for working capital, and the like. It's what they do, their specialty, and some offer personal as well as business loans.

United States Small Business Administration

The SBA does not give loans. It does, however, guarantee long-term loans through other entities to promote small business. By guaranteeing such loans, the SBA enables qualified businesses to acquire loans at a reasonable rate they could not get through other means. The SBA has district offices to help small business owners and start up operators.

Community Development Companies

CDCs are designed to attract business to an area. Most commonly, they are used to develop commercial industrial parks, but this is not always the case. Check your target area for CDCs and have a chat with CDC officials to see if your business might fit their criteria and thus benefit from their efforts.

Life Insurance Companies

Don't worry, we're not talking about taking out a relative. But your relatives may be able to help. Check to see if you or someone you know has a life insurance policy that has "loan value" or "cash value" against which you can borrow (often at a lower rate than commercial enterprises). Many policies, including your own, can provide funding opportunities.

Equity Funding

Equity funding involves selling shares (or stock) in your company, this allowing the investor to become an owner and share in the increase in the company's value. At first blush it sounds great. You give up, for example, 20% of the company to 200 shareholders in exchange for $2 million. You're in business. Life is great.

It is not that easy. Standing in your way is one of the most complicated and harrowing areas of our legal system: The securities laws.

Designed to protect 'widows and orphans' from unscrupulous high pressure securities salesmen, as well as to encourage market efficiency, the securities laws have become a morass of highly technical rules and regulations filled with giant traps for the unwary.

Failing to follow these rules can lead to a right of recession whereby investors are able to demand their money back. It doesn't matter that all the money was already spent on rent and phones and other expenses. If the company can't return the money, guess who is responsible? In many cases where the raising of money has defrauded proverbial widows and orphans, bad actors go to jail.

So how can you raise money with your business plan in this environment?

Believe it or not, our federal and state governments recognize that capital formation, the raising of monies for new and expanding businesses, is a good thing. Capital formation creates jobs and revenue, which, of course, can be taxed. Due to this government self interest there are certain exceptions to the securities laws that make it somewhat easier on entrepreneurs. While a complete discussion of even these exceptions is beyond the scope of this book, there are two rules that readers should know before seeking equity funding.

1. The First Round is Free

The first round of securities sales, also known as the founder's round, is free from the more onerous restrictions of later rounds. Of course, this doesn't give you free reign to misrepresent the company's prospects to anyone. You still have to be truthful, but the document requirements are lessened in the founder's round. As mentioned in other parts of this book, rules change and it is imperative that you seek the advice of qualified legal counsel when securing any funding for your business.

Suppose, for example, a corporation has just been formed to pursue a business opportunity. Ten million shares have been authorized. The founders of the company want to issue themselves 5.1 million shares to assure majority control for the near future. (Issuing 5.1 million shares at the start gives them 51% ownership even when all 10 million shares are eventually used.) They each pay 5¢ a share for their stock raising $255,000 on the sale of 5.1 million shares to get started. Because this is the first issuance of stock and everyone is paying the same price the more comprehensive requirements of Rule 506 (as discussed ahead) are not applicable. In other words, the first bite of the apple is free.

But what if you really need $350,000 to get started? The founders have come up with all they could with the first $255,000. However, another $95,000 would get them through the first 24 months according to projections. If they don't raise the extra $95,000 now, the company will have to stop after 16 months, spend $10,000 to $25,000 on a Rule 506 private placement memorandum and financial audit and start looking for money. Once the company was in business for 24 months the projections had it turning a profit and perhaps not needing any more money. So an additional $95,000 raised now made a great deal of sense.

How can the company raise the additional $95,000 without a great deal of extra professional fees and expenses? By bringing in investors into the first round as founders. As long as everyone pays the same amount of money (5¢ a share) for the same type of stock (in this case Class A common with full voting rights) in the first round the more onerous document requirements don't apply. (But remember, you still cannot advertise this offering, you shouldn't sell to more than a handful of close acquaintances, and you should have each person sign a subscription agreement verifying that they know what they are getting into and that they could lose all their money.) So in this case the company sold an additional 1.9 million shares to friends and family in the founder's issuance. A total of 7 million shares were sold raising the desired $350,000 in the hopes that that amount would be enough for the company to reach profitability. Of course if it didn't, the company could always sell its remaining 3 million shares and could even authorize and issue more shares. But that would have to be in a second, and more expensive, round of funding. For now the company, thanks to the relative ease of the expanded founder's round, had enough money to proceed.

2. Rule 506

In its desire to promote capital formation while at the same time protecting widows and orphans the Securities and Exchange Commission (SEC) of the U.S. Government has put forth rules governing the sale of securities in private companies. Known as exempt offerings, meaning they are free from the really rigorous and very costly requirements of public offerings, they still can be challenging and expensive.

The most common exempt offering is known as Rule 506 of Regulation D. This path is the one most commonly taken if only because it preempts (or supercedes) the pesky and sometimes conflicting requirements under your state's securities laws. Using Rule 506 means you are operating under one law in all states – the federal law.

It is important to note some Rule 506 definitions right from the start.

An accredited investor is a sophisticated individual who has over $1 million in net worth or $200,000 a year in income over the last three years (or $300,000 a year if married). It is the SEC's position that accredited investors, by virtue of their assets and holdings, don't need as great a level of protection as do others. The SEC protects widows and orphans, not idiots. Accredited investors can invest in companies without a great deal of documentation involved.

An unaccredited investor is an individual that falls below the above mentioned net worth or income levels. The SEC believes this person needs more assistance when investing. Under Rule 506 a private placement memorandum (or "PPM") must be prepared disclosing all of the risks involved with the investment. The PPM also lays out issues involving management, strategy and goals. In fact, the PPM is really a legal document that incorporates the business plan. If you are raising money from unaccredited investors for your business, you will most likely use a PPM.

Rule 506 limits the number of unaccredited investors in any one offering to 35. Any investors above that number must be accredited investors. Unaccredited investors are entitled to a full PPM with all the legal disclosures and notices. These documents are usually prepared by well-paid securities attorneys. As well, audited financials must be provided. (If you are brand new with no financial activities to audit, the audit rule can be waived.)

The combination of preparing a full PPM as well as audited financials can be burdensome and costly. Audits have become very expensive to obtain and PPMs have never been cheap. To spend $10,000 to $25,000 for just 35 investors does not add up for many companies. When combined with the fact that many times the unaccredited investors have the most at risk, percentage wise of their net worth, and can become overly anxious and aggressively communicative as a result, many executives decide to limit their offerings to only accredited investors. In this way, no expensive audits or PPMs are needed. A business plan and subscription agreement can suffice.

Nevertheless, in order to protect yourself, you will want the subscription agreement to contain language that states the investor knew what he or she was getting into, they fully appreciated the risks and can afford to lose their entire investment. You also want them to sign a purchaser suitability questionnaire in which they represent they are an accredited investor. Taking these steps and saving the signed agreements will help protect you from an investor claim of whatever sort at a later date.

There is one more important point to note about both a Founder's Round and a Rule 506 Round of funding. Neither allow any sort of advertising or promotion. You can't use radio or TV ads, seminars or mailings of any kind. The exemptions are called private because they are not public. You can't publicly advertise them. Instead, you may only sell to your circle of friends, family and business acquaintances. If your accountant wants to show the investment to a few of his clients, that is okay. If your lawyer wants to mass mail it to all the firm's clients, that is not okay because it is a general solicitation and not allowed.

Again, this is an area to be very careful in as an innocent mistake can still lead to big trouble. Be sure to work with a good securities attorney when it comes to proper investment counsel.

Now that you are ready to sell your equity it is time to appreciate that equity funders have their own set of priorities. Some of these investors may be strangers, others may be family or friends. Some may be putting up money that belongs to a corporation, or an investment fund, while others are investing their own individual hard-earned dollars. Either way, investors want to see a return on that investment. They are most certainly interested in the long-term health and growth of your business because it means long-term and healthy returns on their investments.

Many people who would consider investing a small amount of money in your business (usually family, friends and friends of friends) are concerned about the safety of their investment. They are hoping for some return above their initial investment amount, but they are highly concerned about risk. They are often more concerned about the worst-case scenario of losing their money than they are about the best-case scenario of making big bucks through their willingness to help you get your business off the ground. These types of individuals may never invest in your venture, or any one else's, because of the risk involved. Those that do may have buyer's remorse.

There are a number of investors who are willing to risk their relatively small amount of money in hopes of your business going public or getting sold and becoming that million-dollar success story they are always reading about. They want 10¢ a share to hit $100 a share. These investors are more concerned with the big return on a small investment than they are with losing their investment. They are more comfortable with the gamble than are their counterparts. But some of these gamblers may still worry over their investments. In some cases their concern, which can lead to calls and demands on the company, can be quite a pain.

In all of this, keep your antenna up. If someone strikes you the wrong way, go with your gut and don't let them in as an investor. No matter how much you need the money, you don't need the trouble of an off kilter investor. Please be very cautious as to who you let in.

That said, the cautious investor, the gambler, all investors will want to see detailed information on profits and losses, the market and the potential for growth.

Some corporate investors may have a much higher tolerance for risk. This is because they are more seasoned and professional about analyzing risk. Corporate investors are often looking to invest in businesses that will somehow help their existing companies -- allowing them to enter a new market segment, expand, outmaneuver the competition or any other strategic advantage. These investors are interested in seeing information on the potential of the market, alliances with other companies and the strategic importance of your business in its market and industry. You must be very careful that they are not just looking at your business plan for good ideas. For a discussion of confidentiality and sample confidential disclosure forms, see my book *Buying and Selling a Business*.

Friends and Family

No man is an island, especially in business. Immediate family, crotchety uncles, long-lost cousins -- blood is the color of money for new business. Then there are your friends from school, the kid you bunked with at camp, the folks who cheered you on when you quit that job from hell -- all these friends are fair game as well when you are looking for investors for a new company. The nice thing about friends and family is that they will often cut you a deal -- little or no interest on loans, liberal repayment schedules, or friendly terms. Some won't even ask for partial ownership or stock options. However, the bad thing is that you risk losing those same relationships if anything goes wrong or if there are misunderstandings. Be sure to guard your relationships as closely as your money. Present your business plan to friends and family just as you would any other potential investor and get all agreements in writing. Once again, don't present the opportunity to friends or family members who really shouldn't be investing. Your grief will be doubled if you lose their money.

Private Investors

There are individuals and private companies whose business is investing in entrepreneurial ventures. A challenging economy can certainly weed the herd, but private investors are always on the lookout for investment opportunities. Some can be found in the classifieds or on the Internet, but beware of people you don't know. Some are outright scam artists insisting on upfront fees to review your deals. Never pay an upfront fee to anyone. If they really like the deal they can put up their own time and money just like everyone else. More importantly, if you don't like their ethics or style or even their toupee don't accept their money. You'll have to live with these people for a long time. A snake in the grass will certainly bite you someday.

There are other, less abrasive private investors to worry about as well. These investors will want as much of the company as they can get, for as little as possible. Chances are you need money to move forward. You are vulnerable. You need to remember that these private investors can be very savvy and persuasive. Don't get so caught up in the short-term goal of getting startup capital that you lose sight of your goals and vision for the company. Protect your interests and be sure you are getting a good deal. Having a lawyer by your side can be very helpful in this area.

Venture Capital Firms

Venture capital firms are a useful component in the business engine of growth. They are also hard nosed investors who have earned the not so flattering nick name 'vulture capitalists'. When it comes to 'VCs', you need to be knowledgeable and cautious.

A venture capital firm is a company that raises large amounts of money from individuals and institutions and then invests in startup businesses. Because these firms don't do anything else, they are very interested in the finances of the businesses in which they invest -- so much so that they will usually want significant ownership in the company (and possibly a seat on the board or a place in management) with input on day-to-day decisions. Members of venture capital firms are big on profits and big on growth. Some want to triple their money in 18 months. Others want even greater returns. To do that they'll need a large chunk of your shares and they'll drive your (their) company with the accelerator past the floorboard. In achieving their goals, they've left many a founder behind at the rest stop. Of course, being left behind with 10% ownership of a company whose stock is soaring may not be such a bad result for some. But for others it can be bruising. Be sure to talk to your advisors and other clients of the venture firm you are considering before formalizing a relationship. In many cases a venture firm can be a big help, in others a major hindrance. Be careful.

Yes, you need funding. What price are you willing to pay for it?

Chapter Thirteen

Financial Forecasting

"They know enough who know how to learn."
– Henry Adams

Scott

Scott was clueless when it came to financials and forecasting. Scott knew how to make money at his video production studio, but keeping it was another matter. He was considered one of the best studios in town for video, audio and mixing. He even produced quality still photography shots from videos for publicity purposes. But Scott sensed he was slipping. He grudgingly knew he needed to expand his operations to keep up with the market. But he was having so much trouble tracking his money, so how could he? He was overwhelmed when it came to accounting and bookkeeping and finances in general.

Then one day, two things happened that dramatically changed his course. First, he lost a significant job to a company he considered to be a lesser production house. When he called to find out why he had lost the work, Scott learned that his lowly competitor had expanded their services offered and had upgraded all of their equipment. They could produce a higher quality video at a lower cost. Second, several employee checks had bounced. The employees were not happy. Their NSF payroll checks caused a cascade of late fees and penalties on mortgage, credit card and other payments. One employee quit over it. Scott's valued assistant warned him that such a thing could never happen again.

That was it for Scott. He knew he had to get a handle on his books and then prepare a business plan so he could catch up with the competition. He asked his lawyer for advice on how to proceed. The attorney gave him the name of a consultant named Ron who had helped out another client recently.

Shortly thereafter, Ron visited Scott at his studio. He listened to Scott talk of his frustrations with his accounting and his need for a bank loan to acquire new equipment to keep up with his competitors. Scott was very worried he could never get a bank loan because he didn't have the systems in place to prove that he'd ever be able to repay a loan. At this moment he wasn't even sure whether he could repay a loan or not.

Ron told Scott not to worry. There were plenty of entrepreneurs in his exact situation. With a little help they were able to pull it together, obtain a bank loan and thrive. He would, too.

That was fine, Scott said. But the accounting had become such a problem that he had developed a mental block to it all. When he heard all the financial terms he just tuned them out. He was stressed that he could never comprehend it well enough to talk to a banker.

Ron had the solution to Scott's mental block. They would go through the four main accounting reports and relate them to Scott's business. This way when Scott heard the term, he could equate it to an aspect of his business and be able to talk about it.

Scott agreed to give it a try. Ron identified the four main reports they would be discussing as:

1. Income Statement

2. Cash Flow Statement

3. Balance Sheet

4. Break Even Analysis

Ron could sense Scott's frustration at the mere mention of these terms. So he asked Scott a production question: "What was a snapshot?" After several questions as to why this was relevant to anything at all, Ron got Scott to answer that a snapshot, as in a photograph, was an image in time.

Ron then told Scott that was also what an income statement was: a snapshot of your business at one point in time.

If an income statement is prepared on June 30th, then like a photograph taken on June 30th, it will show you if you are making any money as of June 30th. Scott slowly nodded.

Ron went on to say that in an income statement you bring all of your revenue from sales and other sources into the picture, take out all of your costs, and end up with a snapshot of net income. This is your photo of the amount of profit or loss you have on, for example, June 30th.

Ron went on to say that income statements are also called earning statements or profit and loss statements (P&Ls) but they all provided the same thing: a snapshot of the business on a fixed date in time.

Scott said he was getting the picture, so to speak. Ron laughed and said next was the cash flow statement.

A cash flow statement was movement. It showed where the money came from and where it went. It was different from an income statement, which took a still picture of sales and profits.

Instead, the cash flow statement told you where the cash came from, how it was being used in the company and how it was going out of the company. There was movement to a cash flow statement, Ron explained. It was a video. Scott's eyes lit up. He could visualize the movement.

Ron went on to explain there were two parts to this video. One was called the sources of funds, which tracked not only sales but also loans, line of credit drawdowns and equity investments from investors. It recorded the movement of money into the company.

Part two of the video showed the uses of funds -- the movement of money within the company. This included the costs of goods sold, administrative expenses, loan and interest payments, equipment purchases and dividends or draws paid to the owners.

The result of this movement of cash into the company, around the company and out of the company was called the net change in cash. It was the difference between total funds in and total funds out.

Ron noted that a happy ending to this video would show a positive number and an upward trend. Scott said he was on the edge of his chair to see how his cash flow video ended. Ron agreed but reminded Scott that the cash flow statement didn't have a finite end. Instead it was a measuring tool, a means for improving performance over time. A never-ending video. Scott liked that idea.

A balance sheet was the third report he needed to understand. This matched your assets – the things you owned – with your liabilities – the items you owe on. The result was your total assets.

Scott didn't see how this related to video production. Ron asked him to think about his production work. Ron asked him to think about a mixing job, where you had to lay the audio (the sound) with the video (the image) properly for the production to work. The two had to match and be balanced. Scott saw this clearly.

Ron said this was how Scott should remember a balance sheet. The mix of audio and video into one valuable asset. Or, in accounting terms, the mix of assets with liabilities to equal net worth. Scott saw it, and Ron went on to clarify that just as an income statement was a snapshot of the business, and a cash flow statement was the movement of money, a balance sheet was used to get at the owner's equity or net worth of the business.

The key element of the balance sheet was that it had to balance. In video terms, it couldn't look like the English translation of a Japanese movie where the spoken words didn't match the movement of the actor's lips. Instead, the assets on one side and the liabilities on the other side had to be equal and had to balance.

Ron noted that if you had more assets than liabilities (and hopefully he did), the difference was the net worth of the business. By tracking this regularly, you could see if you were getting richer or poorer.

Scott understood and Ron moved on to the break-even analysis.

Ron guessed that Scott, like almost every other video guy he'd ever met, would love to someday make a big budget Hollywood movie. When Ron asked the question, Scott perked up at the thought.

Ron explained that break-even analysis was like opening night. The movie had been made. Now how many tickets did you have to sell to break even? Scott understood but asked about the distributors and movie houses. They got a cut of every ticket sold.

Ron explained that was factored into the equation. With a movie, you knew on opening night what the fixed costs to make it were. And you knew how much the distributor took out of each ticket, for example, 60%. Similarly, in a business you had fixed costs such as rent, insurance and office costs each month and you had an average gross profit margin on each sale.

Continuing with the movie example, suppose it cost $1,000,000 to make a low budget thriller. That was the fixed cost. The distributor and movie houses were going to keep 60% of each $7.00 ticket sold. Your gross profit margin was 40%. By dividing the $1,000,000 film cost by the 40% you get from each ticket you learn that you need to sell $2.5 million in tickets to bring in the $1 million needed to break even.

Scott clearly understood this and excitedly began talking about a script he'd been working on with a friend. Ron brought him back to reality.

Just as you had opening night for a film, you had the first of the month for your business. You knew what your rent and other fixed expenses were. From there, you had to figure how many things, be it tickets, products or services, you would have to sell and at what percentage of profit to break even for the month.

Ron got Scott to focus on his own business. With rent and all the other fixed expenses it cost him $12,000 a month to keep the doors open. A video production job, after paying for film and supplies, netted him 50% of the monies paid by the client. So, using the break-even equation, Ron told Scott that he needed to bring in $24,000 a month just to break even.

Scott shook his head. There were some months when he came nowhere near that amount. Ron said he needed this tool for bidding on jobs and taking on new business. You needed to know where you were every month, and you had to hold your margins to reach your break-even point before moving into profitability.

Ron summarized the discussion by writing it down on a piece of paper for Scott to remember:

Accounting Term	Production Term	Answers the question:
Income Statement	Snapshot	Am I making money?
Cash Flow Statement	Video	Where did the money move?
Balance Sheet	Audio/Video Mix	What is this worth?
Break Even Analysis	Opening Night	When do I start making money?

Scott appreciated the assistance. His mental block was removed. With Ron's help the financials were brought into order, reasonable income projections were crafted and a bank loan was obtained. Scott went on to profitability, and eventually made his movie.

Bankers and investors will be looking at your plan to see if your business is a good risk. In other words, will your business income allow for timely repayment of borrowed money? One of the ways this risk is analyzed is by reviewing your income projections, which is also known as a pro forma profit and loss forecast. Your income projections report is based on the other four reports we've just discussed. If you are a startup and don't have a prior history, you'll be making all five reports up out of thin air, in which case we must favor reality over creativity.

The income projection is a way for bankers and/or investors to get an idea of what the near future (usually three years, seldom more than five) will hold in terms of income and expenses based on reasonable assumptions of costs and sales. Your assumptions should be based on prior experience and real-world numbers. Don't try to predict the future with a cracked crystal ball. Be realistic.

Obviously a three-year income projection is a pro forma statement and must be backed up by sound reasoning and expertise -- both of which you should have after all your research on industry standards and trends. If you are basing your projections on past performance, be clear about it. But don't just take last year's numbers and shove them into next year's projections. Be sure to take into account changes in the industry, the economy, marketing, competition, efficiency, costs, and the like. If you are basing projections on standards and trends, state where you got your information. Again, be realistic. The people you'll be dealing with will know when you're blowing smoke.

Whereas the cash flow statement records the movement of all cash going in and all cash going out, the income projection looks only at income and deductible expenses. But all parts of your business plan build on each other. The cash flow statement will contain some of the information you need for income projection.

The timeline for an income projection can vary depending on how you are using the plan and what you want to accomplish. But three to five years is the average. But remember that the art of prognostication blurs with distance. Three years is certainly a reasonable timeline because it gives a glimpse of the future without risking too much inaccuracy. But note that different funding entities may prefer other timelines. Don't be put off if someone asks for five years and you've only got three. If you want their money, go back and do five.

As with the overall timeline, the time breakdown of your forecast can vary as well. If you are preparing your plan for management purposes, you may want to show your projections by year. If you are preparing your plan to attract funding, projections by month may work well. But different entities have different preferences, so it is a good idea to check with your target entities ahead of time to find out how they would like your financials laid out.

The basic categories for an income projection are the same as those for the income statement and include:

Income
  Net sales (account for returns, allowances and markdowns)
  Cost of sales (such as inventory, purchases, costs of goods available
    for sale and deduct for inventory)
  Gross profit (cost of sales subtracted from net sales)
Expenses
  Variable (such as advertising, professional fees, packaging costs,
    freight, supplies and parts, payroll -- including overtime and

benefits, repair and maintenance, travel)
Fixed (such as rent, leases, utilities, loan repayment and interest, insurance, depreciation of capital assets, workers' compensation, taxes and licenses and office salaries)
Total
Income from operations (expenses subtracted from gross profit)
Other income (such as interest income)
Other expenses
Net profit or loss before taxes
Taxes (such as sales, real estate, income, inventory and excise)
Net profit or loss after income taxes

Rich Dad Tips

- Financial projections require a high level of financial literacy. If you don't have great expertise, use the creation of your financial projections as a learning experience and hire a CPA or accountant who will teach you the fundamentals of the statements while you prepare them together.

- There are several user friendly accounting programs for small businesses that are great resources for both the financially astute as well as the new business owner. Research the internet for what others have to say about affordable software such as QuickBooks from Intuit.

Forecasting

Forecasting numbers for the future should not be an exercise in wishful thinking. Rather, your forecasts should be based on realistic expectations and real-world experience. However, not all the experience needs to come from you. If you are a brand new business owner, it is a good idea to talk to others or even hire some professionals to help you get the numbers right. If you are an owner of an existing business, try including your managers and department heads when planning for the future. This is called bottom-up forecasting.

Bottom-up forecasting uses the knowledge of the frontlines to predict as accurately as possible the future needs of your business. Managers and department heads can plan ahead for the needs of their teams and give the data to you to approve and compile. These front-liners know what equipment will need to be replaced next year, what positions will need to be added and how many training programs need to be added. Your sales team should have a good idea as to where sales are going and what trends might change the path you are currently on, and the like. Each manager or department head can look at the next few years month by month and come up with a realistic forecast. You can add all those forecasts together to prepare a picture of the future of your business as a whole. Of course, your front-liners cannot accurately predict everything that will be needed in the coming three years, but they may have insight you don't.

Top-down forecasting is planning for the future with the end in mind. It starts with your goals for three years out and back tracks the steps it will take to get there. You start with the big picture -- the industry -- and your goals within it. With your market share goal you can figure your projected revenue. From there you work your way down the table, filling in exact numbers where you can and making your best predictions where you can't. Still, these are not guesses. Even the advertising section (one of the most variable sections of your projection) can be worked out logically. You know where you stand with the competition and the industry norms. So you know if you will need to spend more or less than the norm in order to increase your piece of the pie. How much more is a little murkier, but your Marketing section analysis should be able to guide you.

Top-down forecasting allows you to work your goals into your company's expectations of the future. It also allows for some spin, but keep it real.

Now to drive home the financials and forecasting of financials, we're going to review the four reports again and look at some new beneficial ratios to use. If you feel like you've had enough of all the numbers, feel free to go on to the next chapter.

Cash Flow Statement – Cash is King!

Money comes in; money goes out. The difference between the two is your profit or loss. Put it all on paper along with a timeline and you have a basic cash flow statement (or budget). This means you put down how much money you expect from whom (by category -- sales, loans, etc.) and when (by date, week, month or quarter), how much money you will need to pay out (bills, debts and expenses) to whom and when.

In *Rich Dad's Guide to Investing*, Robert Kiyosaki wrote, "Cash flow management is a fundamental and essential skill if a person truly wants to be successful in the B quadrant. Many small business owners fail because they do not know the difference between profit and cash flow."

If preparation of the report seems daunting, try breaking it down into easily digestible pieces. Create separate budgets for revenues (real and/or projected), cost of sales, fixed expenses and variable expenses. You may also want to create a table of all your sources of incoming cash as well as one for all outgoing cash. You don't have to include all this information in your plan (the table may contain detail better left under wraps). Then you can use these tables to figure out where the money is going to come from to pay the bills each month if cash in and cash out don't exactly coincide. And there's your timeline.

Your table or spreadsheet for cash flowing into your business can include categories such as:

Amount of cash you have available for the business

Sale revenues (broken out by sales, service, accounts receivable, collections and deposits)

Interest income

Any sales of long-term assets

Liabilities (such as loans)

Equity (such as owner investments, sales of stock or venture capital)

Your table or spreadsheet for cash flowing out of your business can include categories such as:

    Startup costs (including business licenses)
    Inventory purchases
    Controllable expenses (such as freight, packaging and advertising)
    Fixed expenses (such as rent, utilities and insurance)
    Long-term purchase assets
    Liabilities (such as paying back loans)
    Owner equity (money you take out as an owner)

You can prepare a statement for any stretch of time you want, but remember that the farther out you project, the more you risk losing accuracy. It is best to stick to one fiscal year, beginning with the start of the current fiscal year and stepping month to month to the end of that same fiscal year. To improve accuracy, keep revising the statement (monthly is ideal) to reflect reality and your ever-increasing expertise.

The timeline will help you plan for the time lag often involved with collection of receivables and will allow you to time collections so that you are not caught short when bills come due. For example, your office supply store likely experiences an influx of cash during August and September because of the back-to-school frenzy. But your big bills may come significantly later in the year. Plan accordingly.

The cash flow statement (like most budgets) only includes real money (cash in, cash out). It does not include non-cash transactions (such as amortization or depreciation).

The traditional format of a cash flow statement has the total for the year and the subtotals for each month in 13 columns (vertical) with column labels across the top. The rows (horizontal) show the beginning balance and the amount of cash in and cash out by source with the sources listed on the far left. The table (or spreadsheet) will be easier to understand if you break categories into subcategories when you can.

Here is an example of a detailed Cash Flow Statement:

Total (this row is the Total for each category by column)
Beginning Cash Balance (enter under Month 1)
Cash Receipts
      Sales Revenues
            Cash Sales
            Receivables
      Sale of Long-Term Assets
      Interest Income
Total Cash Available (add the Beginning Cash Balance to all Cash Receipts)

Cash Payments
      Cost of Sales
            Material
            Labor
            Purchases
      Controllable Expenses
            Supplies
            Salaries
            Freight
            Packaging
            Advertising
            Miscellaneous
      Fixed Expenses
            Rent/Lease
            Utilities
            Office Salaries
            Licenses/Permits
            Insurance
            Advertising
            Miscellaneous
      Loan Payments
      Interest Payments

Long-Term Asset Payments

Taxes

Federal Income Tax

Other Taxes

Owner Draws

Total Cash Paid Out (add Costs of Sales, Controllable Expenses, Fixed Expenses, Loan Payments, Interest Payments, Long-Term Asset Payments, Taxes and Owner Draws)

Balance (Subtract Total Cash Paid Out from Total Cash Available -- put negatives in brackets)

Incoming Loans (loan money coming in)

Equity Deposits (deposits to be made)

Ending Balance (add the numbers for each month; this number should be the same as the total for month 12)

An example of a Pro Forma Cash Flow Statement is found in the Appendix.

The following is an example of a simplified Cash Flow Statement:

Cash Flow Statement

Sources of Cash

Sales

Other Sources

Interest

Short-term Borrowings

Total Cash In

Uses of Cash

COGS

SG&A

Interest

Taxes

Equipment Purchase

Debt Principal Payments

Dividends

Total Cash Out

NET CHANGE IN CASH
Beginning Cash on Hand
Ending Cash on Hand

If you are writing your plan for an existing business, putting together the cash flow statement is reasonably easy. You know what came in and what went out in the past (you reported it on your taxes, didn't you?), so it doesn't take a lot of thought to add figures for the upcoming period as well. However, don't be complacent. Take advantage of seeing all these numbers on paper and try to envision them as if you were not the business owner. Can you see anywhere where you can make future changes that might improve your bottom line?

If you are preparing your plan for a startup business, the exercise of preparing a cash flow statement requires more thought. But in conjunction with preparing the other sections, you should have enough knowledge of your business, market and industry to be able to project reasonable costs and sales figures. If you don't, or if you find it difficult to prepare a reasonable projection, you may want to rethink your other sections and go back to researching.

Balance Sheets

A balance sheet (also known as a statement of financial position) is a balance of your company's finances. It presents data on assets, liabilities and net worth. As you may already know, assets are anything of monetary value owned by the business. Liabilities are company debts. Net worth is capital -- the worth of your equity as owner. When you add liabilities and net worth, you get a total for assets. Generally accepted accounting principals link these three due to their mathematical relationship. A positive net worth means assets outweigh liabilities; a negative net worth means liabilities outweigh assets.

Balance sheets always use the same format no matter what the business is. All professionals expect this format. Anyone can read them and easily compare one to another. Due to the ease of interpretation of this format, balance sheets are relatively simple to create:

Assets are anything of value owned by or legally due to the company and fall into four categories:

1. Current: those that can be converted to cash within a year (such as cash, checking and savings accounts, accounts receivable, short-term investments, prepaid expenses and inventory from raw materials to finished products)
2. Long-term: investments such as stocks, bonds and special savings accounts to be kept for at least a year
3. Fixed: resources not meant for resale (such as land, buildings, improvements, equipment, vehicles and furniture)
4. Other: assorted assets that typically are unique to a business' circumstances

Liabilities fall into two categories:

1. Current: payable within one operating cycle (such as notes, taxes, interest, payroll accrual and accounts payable)
2. Long-term: mortgages, vehicles, notes and the like (take the current part due subtracted from the remaining balance)

Net worth or owner equity is given according to the legal structure of your business.

Corporations use the total invested by owners or stockholders added to retained earnings (after dividends are paid).

Partnerships, LLC's or sole proprietorships use the original investment of owners added to earnings after withdrawals.

A sample projected balance sheet is found in the Appendix.

Balance sheets should be prepared on a regular basis, not just when you are preparing a business plan. The balance sheet can help you spot trends and plug cash leaks before they sink your company.

If you are preparing your plan for a new business, you may want to include a personal balance sheet of your personal finances instead of a business balance sheet to show your ability to handle money. Then again you may not want to do so in order to show that you value your privacy.

Income Statement

The income statement (also known as a profit and loss statement or statement of operations) reveals your business profitability at a set point in time. What your business has spent (and what it was spent on) is combined with what your business has brought in (and from where) to tell you whether you made money or not.

Preparation of the income statement is best done on a monthly as well as yearly basis. You really don't want to wait a year to see if you are making money. The data for your income statement should be readily available from your company records.

Again, there is a standard, expected format for your financial data. The income statement should include:

Income
>	Net sales (returns and allowances subtracted from gross sales)
>	Costs of goods sold
>	Gross profit (costs of goods sold subtracted from net sales)
>	Other

Expenses
>	Direct, controllable, variable (those associated with sales)
>	Indirect, fixed, office, overhead (those associated with administration)
>	Other

Net profit/loss before income taxes
Income taxes
Net profit/loss after income taxes

Here is a sample of a detailed Income Statement:

Income Statement for 20___	JAN	FEB	MAR	APR	MAY	JUN	JUL	AUG	SEP	OCT	NOV	DEC
INCOME												
Net Sales												
Costs of Goods Sold												
Gross Profit												
Other												
EXPENSES												
Variable												
Advertising												
Professional Fees												
Freight												
Parts												
Supplies												
Miscellaneous												
Fixed												
Rent												
Utilities												
Insurance												
Permits												
Miscellaneous												
TOTAL EXPENSES												
OPERATION INCOME												
OTHER INCOME												
OTHER EXPENSES												
PRE-TAX INCOME												
INCOME TAXES												
NET INCOME												

Here is an example of a simplified Income Statement:

Income Statement for 20___	
Gross Sales	
Cost of Goods Sold	
Gross Profit	
Expenses	
Net Profit Before Taxes	
Taxes	
Net Profit/Loss	

The income statement can help you track the effectiveness of your plans by showing how expenses and sales are affecting profits or losses. It will also help you plan for variations in sales volumes from month to month. Though you only need one year's worth of info for the business plan, compare income statements over a period of years can help you see longer-term trends and therefore can help you to plan accordingly.

Break-Even Analysis

As discussed, a break-even analysis answers the question of how much your business will need to sell in order to cover its costs. For example, if you sell copy machines, the break-even analysis enables you to figure out exactly how many copiers you need to sell in order to pay all your bills. Add one more copier to the mix and you suddenly see profit.

The analysis is a good one for entrepreneurs because it encourages an in-depth understanding of costs. The analysis is a good one for lenders and investors because it says a lot about whether or not you, as writer of the plan, are realistic in your assumptions.

The break-even point is the dream of any entrepreneur. It is that point at which you can start to breathe a little easier. It is the point when you start to think maybe going into business for yourself was a good decision. It is the beginning of stability. It is the point too many businesses never reach. But numerically, it is the point at which your fixed and variable expenses (including costs of sales) are met by your product and/or service sales. You won't be making a profit, but you will no longer be taking a loss either.

You can display this point in a number of ways in your business plan. In either graph or table form, you can show dollars of expense compared to dollars of revenue or even dollars of expense compared to units of production (in either products or services). Either way you decide to show the information, your income projection can be the source.

If you decide to use a mathematical presentation, you can find the exact break-even point with a simple formula:

$$\text{breakeven} = \text{fixed expenses} + (1\text{-variable expenses} / \text{sales})$$

To create your own break-even diagram, you must first plot your fixed costs and variable costs. Label your vertical axis as costs (in dollars). Then label the horizontal axis as sales (in dollars). Your fixed costs will form a straight horizontal line across the graph because your fixed costs will stay constant even as your sales increase. Your variable costs line will increase as sales increase. The line formed by plotting variable costs on top of fixed costs will create your total cost line. Now you must add your revenue. Because revenue is income that increases as sales increase, your revenue line will be drawn at a forty-five degree angle on the chart. The point at which your revenue line and your total cost line meet is marked as your break-even point.

Break Even Analysis	Month 1	Month 2	Month 3	Month 4	Month 5	Month 6	Month 7
Sales	20000	22000	24000	26000	28000	30000	32000
Costs Variable	12000	13000	14000	14000	15000	16000	17000
Costs Fixed	10000	10000	10000	10000	10000	10000	10000
Fixed + Variable Costs	22000	23000	24000	24000	25000	26000	27000
Net	-2000	-1000	0	2000	3000	4000	5000

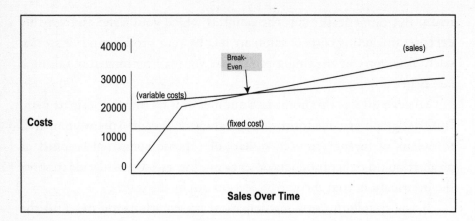

Because the graphic presentation is such a great way to express complicated data for a visually-focused society and the numerical presentation is so great for bankers and other number-focused types, you may choose to present your data in both formats (might as well cover your bases) or pick and choose and customize for your particular audience.

Ratios and Margins

When potential investors begin their task of analyzing your business for risk and feasibility, they bring experience and expertise to bear on your business plan. It's not simply a matter of whether or not they like your idea or whether or not they have the money to give. Nor is it a matter of how personally persuasive you are. What it comes down to is whether or not they think your business proposal, as presented in your business plan, is feasible. In other words, can your business make money?

One of the ways experienced financial decision-makers make their decisions is through the analysis of ratios. Just as the term applies, ratio analysis involves taking numbers from the financial tables and comparing one to another. Which numbers are chosen and how they are combined tells a lot about different aspects of the business under scrutiny.

Most ratios are not analyzed in a vacuum either. Ratios are commonly compared to one another in a historical, competitive and/or budgetary context. By comparing current figures with those of the past, decision-makers can get a feeling for mobility and trends within the company. By comparing figures for one company to those of competing companies, decision-makers can get a feeling for where the company stands in the competitive hierarchy of its industry. By comparing real figures to budgeted figures, decision-makers can see how well you have budgeted. This last comparison usually comes into play after funding has been granted. It is a good way for investors to stay on top of a company's promises. It is also a great way for you or your management team to learn to refine your budgeting abilities.

Knowledge of ratios on your part is akin to learning to speak the language of potential investors. It gives you a chance to see what impressions your financials will make on decision-makers. It also gives you a valuable management tool. By tracking your ratios, you can spot trends, strengths, weaknesses and potential roadblocks.

Following are some of the most commonly used ratios.

Liquidity Ratios

The current ratio and the quick ratio are two examples of liquidity ratios. The current ratio is used to determine liquidity of an existing business by dividing current assets by current liabilities. If the current ratio is greater than 1.0, then the business has a chance of being able to pay its short-term bills. The larger the number, the better the chance of paying the bills. If that number is less than 1.0, the business may be in rough water. However, decision-makers will also take into account industry norms. If a ratio of 4.0 is the average for an industry, that current ratio of 1.0 is not nearly as good as it would be in an industry with an average of, say, 1.5.

The quick ratio (also called the acid test) is a measurement of liquidity without inventory being calculated in. It is current assets (not including inventory) divided by current liabilities. Comparing the quick ratio to the current ratio gives decision-makers an idea of how dependent liquidity is upon inventory.

Debt Management Ratios

Debt management ratios include the debt ratio and the times interest earned ratio (TIE). The debt ratio is a measure of risk in that it shows how well the company's assets support its monetary obligations. The debt ratio is found by dividing total debt (including long-term debt, short-term debt and current liabilities) by total assets. A high debt ratio means high risk to potential investors.

The TIE measures how well earnings cover interest and can be found by dividing earnings before interest and taxes by interest. The higher the number, the more times earnings can cover interest, thus the safer the investment.

Asset Management Ratios

Inventory turnover and average collection period (ACP) are both examples of asset management ratios. The inventory turnover ratio measures how often your company gets rid of and restocks an average-sized inventory. It is measured by dividing costs of goods sold by inventory. A higher number is better because higher numbers mean you are more quickly going through your inventory. This means fewer of your business dollars are tied up in inventory. Inventory can cost you in storage, taxes, insurance and interest as well as time. Inventory and time are not friends. As time passes, inventory can become outdated, unpopular or even unsafe.

ACP measures how long it takes to collect on sales on credit. When you sell on credit, there will be a lag time. That lag time is measured by the ACP (also known as "days sales outstanding" and the "receivables cycle") and is found by dividing accounts receivable by sales and multiplying the total by 360. Obviously you want that number to be as small as possible. Ideally, you want it as close to your company's terms of sale as you can get it. If the number exceeds your terms of sale significantly (greater than 30 percent is usually a problem), you show that you are not being as strict with your credit choices as you should be or there is significant customer dissatisfaction. Neither is going to endear you to potential investors. While you may have most of your receivables paid promptly, a few very old accounts can skew this ratio. Take into account the odds of ever getting payment from those very old accounts and decide whether or not to write them off.

Profitability Ratios

Profitability ratios include return on sales (ROS), return on asset (ROA) and return on equity (ROE). The ROS ratio is the most basic measurement of profitability and says something about how well you can keep down costs and expenses. Divide net income by sales and, voila, you have profitability (at least on paper).

The ROA ratio similarly says something about how well you use invested assets and is found by dividing net income by total assets.

The ROE ratio builds on the ROA by taking leverage into account and is found by dividing net income by equity. Debt affects ROA and ROE in that the two will be close if debt is small. But when debt grows large, ROE is higher than ROA when the company is doing well and lower when the company is doing poorly.

Financial History/Loan Application

A good indicator of where you're going in business is where you've been. One of the best ways to reassure investors of future success is through showing past success. If you are writing your plan for an existing business, you will include information on your business from startup to present. Put this first in The Financials section; it is your loan application. But prepare it last. Preparation of all the other financial documents will greatly help you in preparation of the financial history.

Even if you are not preparing your plan for investment purposes, this exercise will help in your management practices by helping you look at your business from a big-picture perspective.

The Financial History subsection is a summary. Summarize the data from the other sections and reference those sections accordingly. The following are some of the categories usually summarized in this section:

Assets

Liabilities

Net Worth

Contingent Liabilities

Inventory Detail

Revenues

Expenses

Real Estate Holdings

Stocks

Bonds

Legal Structure

Insurance

Audit Information

If you are writing your plan for a new business, you may want to include information on your personal financial history and status (including a personal finance balance sheet with information on assets: cash, life insurance cash value, trust deeds, personal property, mortgages, real estate, stocks, bonds, mutual funds, accounts receivable, notes receivable; liabilities: unsecured loans, credit card debt, revolving credit debt, notes and deeds, loans secured by personal property, loans against life insurance; net worth; annual income; and annual living expenses). This information will help potential investors see how well you handle money.

Keep in mind that the personal financial history combined with the information you will include in your loan application (provided by institutions upon request) needs to be verifiable and accurate, just as it would if you were providing information on an existing business' financial history.

Uses of Funds

It would be nice if your promise to pay someone back was all it took to get funding for your business. It would be nice if there were institutions or individuals who would write you a blank check to pursue your dreams. But it's not likely. Most institutions and individuals want to know exactly what you plan on doing with their money. And keep that straight: until you pay it back, it is their money.

The best place to start with how you will use the funds you are requesting (if that is the purpose of the plan), is to provide a summary of your business' financial needs. If you are preparing the plan for management purposes only, you will want to skip this section.

The summary of financial needs and the uses of funds can both be short and to the point. An example is found in the Appendix. The first is a simple statement of what you need. Working capital, growth capital and equity capital are the three broad categories of funds. The main difference between the three is in how quickly you will be expected to repay the money. Working capital loans are usually for only a year, growth capital loans are for a few years (usually no more than seven) and equity capital is usually repaid through a stake in the business (which means the payback could be slow in coming, but it may continue to pay over the long haul above and beyond the initial investment).

Be specific as to what you need the funds for. Are you looking for a loan to buy equipment or pay for training? Are you looking for an investor to take on a significant portion of startup costs?

Be specific as to how much you need and how it will be disbursed. If you are buying equipment, for example, list how much that equipment will cost, along with the exact make and model. If you are investing in training, list how much it will cost, how long it will take and who will be doing the training. Give the details it will take for a lender to determine whether or not the investment will increase profit. In fact, if you have data on how profit will be increased (and you should), include that in this section as well.

Assumptions

Not even numbers are concrete in today's world. There is always a bias, whether conscious or not. The purpose of the Assumptions subsection is to explain to readers how you chose your numbers. It is the section readers turn to in order to interpret the biases of the preparer. Assumptions answer the all-important question, "Why?" Why did you decide, for example, you could double your sales in two years? If readers don't know your reasoning, they cannot make an educated decision as to the validity of your numbers. Your assumptions are yet another chance to convince your readers.

If you are preparing your business plan in order to attract investment, you definitely need this section. If you are preparing your plan for management purposes, you might leave it out if it's only for your own use. However, if the plan will be used by others or if you are preparing it for the edification of others in your business, you might want to keep it in. With your assumptions in mind, others within your company are better able to meet goals because they know what is behind those goals. For example, if your income projection states that you plan to double your sales within two years, it would be nice for your sales staff to know how you think that is possible. Is there new technology in the offing? Is a piece of proprietary information finally snaking its way through the approval process? Do you plan an expansion? All good information for your staff to know.

As for format, some plans include the assumptions as footnotes at the bottom of each of the financial tables, some include them as a separate page within each table's subsection and yet others have one separate subsection devoted to explaining all the assumptions that went into all the financials. Choose the format that works best for your business.

Don't get lazy with this subsection and never assume any of the numbers are self-explanatory. Discussions about your plan may occur months after you have prepared your numbers and you might actually forget why, for example, you thought you could double sales within two years. Don't get stuck fumbling for explanations in a loan or investment meeting. If the assumptions are on paper, you can refer to them. If they aren't, you could end up losing the trust of those whose money you are trying to finagle. Why risk it?

Rich Dad Tips

- Know that your investors want to see how much "skin in the game" you have. Keep your salaries as low as possible to show that you are investing "sweat equity."

- Also know that your investors will want your overhead kept low. They want to see their money spent on the business, not on the office surroundings.

Chapter Fourteen

Presenting the Plan

"Thoughts are but dreams till their effect be tried."
– William Shakespeare

Joe and Jessica

Joe had created a business plan for a new gourmet mustard venture. He had spent a great deal of time developing the business initially and very little time putting together a business plan itself.

It took Joe a good long while to learn the importance of the look of the plan. It almost cost him everything.

Joe's plan was a visual mess. The margins were only half an inch wide. Joe had learned in school that wide margins on term papers meant you didn't have anything to say. In the world of academia, the narrower the margins the more words per page. More words per page meant more content, which to his professors meant more work went into the effort. And by this measure (instead of an actual reading in some cases) a better grade was received. And so consequently Joe felt that with narrow margins and a cramped style the brilliance of his plan would be revealed.

Instead, the opposite was true. (White space is your friend.) The first venture capitalist to receive the plan took one look at the tightly spaced and crowded first page and set the whole thing aside. All Joe received was a letter saying the investment didn't fit their profile. He never learned it was the presentation of the plan itself that didn't fit their standards.

The second venture capitalist to receive the plan was a stickler for consistency, neatness and grammar. Joe's plan was inconsistent in the formatting of tables, charts and section headings. It was stapled together in a fairly sloppy fashion. Joe had not bothered to spell check the content. By the time the second venture capitalist saw his second spelling error he had had enough. The whole plan was again set aside. Joe again received a letter saying the investment did not fit their profile.

Joe was perplexed. He had done a great deal of work putting everything in place. He was ready to start shipping cases and cases of the product. He felt like he wasn't getting a straight answer. He wanted to know why the venture guys didn't relish his gourmet mustard.

One of Joe's friends offered to hook him up with a venture capitalist who would give him a straight and honest appraisal of the plan. Joe jumped at the offer and over-nighted the plan out that afternoon.

In three days Joe met with Jessica, a well dressed, no nonsense professional investor. Jessica got right to the point. Joe's plan was a disaster. It was difficult to read because it was too cramped and without any relieving white space.

It was a jumble of type styles and inconsistent formats. The binding with off-centered staples was not neat or professional. Jessica said the entire product reflected poorly on Joe and his business. And in a game where first impressions are crucial, Joe's current first impression would never lead to a second one.

Joe was disappointed but thanked Jessica for her candor. He muttered he would probably lose his orders for 100,000 cases.

Jessica immediately picked up on the comment. What 100,000 case order? Joe elaborated that he had received several purchase orders from the likes of Safeway, Wal-Mart and others. The buyers loved this gourmet mustard and were awaiting shipment.

Jessica asked Joe why the purchase orders weren't included in the supporting materials? Joe didn't realize the documents themselves were important. He had mentioned the orders at the bottom of page 27. Jessica curtly told Joe he was hiding his light under a bushel. Orders of that magnitude should be mentioned on page one and attached as supporting material exhibits.

Joe smiled. Did she think he had something? Jessica was now tearing through the financials, the management section and all her other favorite parts of a business plan. Jessica was starting to appreciate the opportunity in front of her.

As it turned out, Jessica's firm invested in Joe's business. And in the process, and very fortunately, Joe came to fully appreciate the importance of plan presentation and the inclusion of important supporting materials.

The first impression many people will get of your business is in your plan's appearance. Do you think a potential investor or lender will look differently at a business plan that is neatly bound and formatted for ease of understanding compared to one that is written margin to margin with a light green Magic Marker? What impression do you want to give?

Here are a few hints for a good-looking plan:

- Use white (or very light-colored) paper.

- Margins should be at least one inch (but less than two inches) all the way around.

- Font styles should be kept to a minimum (no more than three).

- Colors should be used conservatively (photos and complicated graphics are exceptions). Black print and one or two accent colors is best.

- Pages should be printed on one side only.

- The entire document should be single-spaced with double spaces between paragraphs.

- Don't be afraid of white space. (It relieves the eyes and is less strenuous for the reader.)

- Use bullet points whenever you can.

- Be consistent with formatting of tables, graphs, charts, titles and section headings.

- Use neat, professional binding -- no staples.

- Use a spell-checker.

- Get someone you trust to look through and read the plan. (Ask for their constructive criticism.)

* Include a table of contents at the beginning and an index at the end.

Your cover sheet should include all the information a reader will need to get a hold of you (company name, address and phone number; names, titles, addresses and phone numbers of owners) as well as the company logo, the date the plan was prepared and the name of the person who prepared it.

Rich Dad Tips

- The plan's appearance reflects your commitment to creating a winning business.

- The plan's content is far more important than its appearance, but it won't be read if it doesn't look professional.

Length

It's ironic that it takes a 200 page book to explain how to write a succinct business plan. Typical business plans average between 20 to 40 pages, including support materials. On the surface, it may seem unnecessary to do all the research and planning and organization we suggest, but think of your business plan as a crucible. The research, planning and organization are the components you focus on in order to create a successful business. A winning business plan maps out the keys to a successful business and addresses its unique aspects of your business in a way that will serve your unique temperament, goals and experience while simultaneously meeting the needs of investors and financiers.

So how long should your business plan be? Simple -- as long as it needs to be. How do you know how long it needs to be? You do the preliminary footwork. This book is an excellent first step. Then start writing. As you write it all out, you'll get a sense of how long feels right. And again, have trusted friends review your work. They'll help you determine which areas need to be fleshed out and which ones need to be pared down.

Presentation

Business plans are meant to be seen. Whether you wrote your plan to attract funding or to help with management, you will need to show the plan to someone. And, for review in the next chapter, how you present the plan can vary from country to country.

If you wrote your business plan in order to attract funding and/or investment, you will need to get the plan into the hands of the people who can decide whether or not to give you money. Most of us are uncomfortable when it comes to talking about money. Many of us were taught that it is rude to talk about something so crass. But if you want to someone to give you a loan or invest in your company, you will have to get over your upbringing because you can't just mail out your plan and hope for the best.

If you want loan or investment approval you will need to take meetings and present your plan. Don't think that just having the meeting and leaving the plan for the decision-makers to read will cut it. Don't leave something as important as your business' future to chance. Decision-makers may promise to read your plan and give it consideration, but you can't be sure they actually will. The only way to be sure that your potential investors or lenders get your message is to present it.

The presentation of your business plan should be a business meeting, a formal presentation. Even if the potential investors are your parents and your little brother, you want to present your plan in a serious and professional manner. (Remember, you can't advertise for people to come to this meeting.) But for your pre-existing audience, your friends and family and any professionals you've been in touch with, you may want to use a conference room. This room can be at the potential investor or lender's office. If not and you lack the facilities, try borrowing space from a friend or renting a conference room. You may want to use presentation equipment, such as a computer/projector for your PowerPoint presentation. You should give your audience hard copies of your plan as well. When is up to you.

You can have the plan delivered before the meeting so that your audience will have time to formulate questions, though you run the risk of them making a negative decision before you have a chance to highlight all your positive points. Try having the plan delivered just the day before the meeting so your audience can become familiar with the plan, but it unlikely to make a decision. Or you can hand out the plan at the beginning of the meeting, though you run the risk of your audience reading while you are trying to present. Either way, have copies of your presentation slides to hand out so your audience can follow along.

Your slides and their corresponding handouts should be short, ideally bullet-points, and be in the same visual style as your plan. Your presentation should be less formal than your plan in that you don't want to just sound like you are reading. Try to make it as much like a story as you possibly can. Practice your presentation and get feedback from people you trust to give you honest opinions before you go before people who can make or break your business. Keep in mind that your audience can read -- your slides and your handouts -- so you don't have to. Let your slides be reminders for your talk. Let them remind you what points you want to make and then expand from there.

If you wrote your business plan to aid in management, who sees the plan will depend on your business, your style and your goals. Obviously, if the whole business is comprised of you and your spouse, there don't need to be a lot of secrets. But if yours is a business with a rigid hierarchy with decisions made only at the top level, you may want to limit access. You may choose to share your plan with management only or show employees on a need-to-know basis. You might distribute a version of the plan (say, a version without financial detail, but perhaps with graphs and percentages instead) or you could include sections of the plan in your employee manual. It is entirely up to you. Odds are you will need to consider the twin needs of protecting sensitive information and building a sense of ownership and only you know how to do so.

While people involved with money will have a pretty good idea why you are showing them your business plan, employees might not. You might include your business plan presentation as part of a company retreat or have a special meeting just for the plan. Maybe you want to introduce the plan to everyone at once or department by department. Wherever you choose to have your plan unveiled, be sure you are present. You may choose to deliver the entire message yourself or you might be better served using a team approach with appropriate managers discussing different sections. Again, it comes down to your particular approach and your particular business. Regardless, be sure to explain what a business plan is and how it should be used, why you are showing it and what you expect listeners to do with it. Similarly, if you use the plan as part of your training program for new employees, be sure that they are not just handed the plan cold, but are given the same message you gave the others.

As your business and your business knowledge grows, take some time to check back in with employees to see how the plan is being used and how employees feel it is working. Get suggestions and comments from employees and then use that input to improve the plan. Let the plan work as a road map, a checkpoint and a management tool.

Your plan is a living document

A business plan is an ever-changing, never-completed document. It is always in a state of revision. As time passes, expertise grows, markets change, customer bases alter and technology continues onward. Anyone who reads your plan should get the most up-to-date and complete information you are capable of providing. This means that even after you write the last section of your plan, you need to continue to study the markets and stay abreast of industry, market and economic trends. Just as your business will be in a constant state of flux, so too should your plan be.

Anticipating Problems

Ideally, any business plan, whether written for management purposes or to attract funding, will help anticipate problems that could strike your company. Are costs of supplies going up? Is technology getting cheaper? Is competition increasing or decreasing? What is the motion (if any) of your labor pool? What advertising trends seem to be coming around again? Where is the economy in its current cycle? Are your best-selling products peaking or are they on their downward slide? Which products are showing new strength? Use your plan to draft alternate budgets so you will have some sort of roadmap if good times get bad or bad times get better. Use your plan to assess whether or not your current circumstances (good or bad) are short-term or long-term.

Supporting Materials

Supporting materials are all the documents that can help convince readers of your business plan that your business is worth their time and/or money. As we will discuss in the next chapter, these materials are vital to have in certain countries. The documents should be introduced or referenced in the text of the previous sections so that they can stand-alone in this section. These documents should need no introductory or explanatory text in this section and therefore can be simply arranged and attached to the final plan or offered as a separate document to serious investors or appropriate personnel.

As you go through the process of writing your business plan, you will think of a host of materials that can help you make the argument (to yourself, your management team or potential lenders and investors) that your business is a good risk. These documents give credence to your arguments and they back up your numbers. They help show how you came to your decisions and how you will make your plan work. As you prepare the plan you should keep a notebook close by to jot down the supporting documents you reference in other sections or that you think you might want to include. Be sure you include every document that you mention in your plan. Don't make your readers search for the information they need in order to make an informed decision (ideally, the positive decision you want them to make).

Some of the support materials you should consider include:

Resumes: Ideally, resumes are one page and include work history, education, professional affiliations and honors and special skills. Include resumes for all owners/partners and corporate officers (whatever applies to your corporate entity). Remember, in certain countries titles are very important and are best included.

Letters of Reference: Your letters of reference can come from past investors, lenders or business acquaintances (people you've worked for or with, suppliers, distributors, etc) or from non-business acquaintances (but avoid letters from friends or relatives) and should be assessments of your business skills.

Personal Finances: While some practitioners suggest including a balance sheet of your personal financial history as well as that of other owners/partners, I am not keen on it. Keep your personal information as private as possible.

Leases: Include any lease agreements you have for your business (such as those for buildings, vehicles, equipment, etc.).

Contracts: Include any contracts for your business (such as loans, purchase agreements, service contracts, even maintenance agreements). Remember Joe's 100,000 case gourmet mustard order. That type of business validation is well placed in this section.

Other Legal Documents: Include any other pertinent legal documents such as copyrights, patents, trademarks, insurance policies, and articles of incorporation.

Other Attachments: Include any other documents or information that you have referenced in the body of your plan but that do not fall into any of the above categories. These would include demographic information, maps and the like.

Depending on your business and the information available, you might also consider attaching:

> Glossary of industry terms
>
> Product information
>
> Additional or more specific marketing data
>
> Marketing materials (brochures, catalogs, etc.)
>
> Financial analyst reports
>
> Newspaper or magazine articles
>
> Company history
>
> Press releases
>
> Web pages

Not all plans will need the same information. Those written for management purposes will not need the resumes, letters of reference, or credit reports. Even plans written to attract funding will differ as different lenders or investors will want to see different information. It is best to prepare as much information as you can so that you can easily tailor copies of your plan for various readers and institutions.

And, as we shall see in the next chapter, plans may be tailored for different countries and cultures.

Chapter Fifteen

Business Plans
Around the World

"When doing business in Rome, do business as the Romans"
– Anonymous

As business becomes more global, it becomes even more important to appreciate how local it remains. This is to say that there is not one global standard for doing business: How you conduct a meeting, How you present your business plan, How you negotiate a deal will be subject to the culture and business traditions in your host country.

Just because they do it one way in St. Paul, Minnesota, doesn't mean that's how it's done in Sao Paulo, Brazil. You can either understand, appreciate and embrace the differences or you can be culturally tone deaf, offend your hosts and go home without a deal.

As developing economies continue to advance, as funding sources arise around the world and as business plan competitions become open to all in every nation, it may make sense for you to be open to global opportunities. Which, ironically, means you'll have to become attuned to local business customs. For those of you who are certain that you won't do business beyond your own city, much less your own country, you may want to skip ahead to the next chapter. But before you go, consider one point. The information in this chapter may help you be a better business person where you are. There is a lot of wisdom in the business traditions that have developed over thousands of years in other cultures. Maybe you will glean one nugget of information that suits your own personal style. Maybe that nugget leads to the funding of your business plan. To skip ahead or read on is your call.

We must distinguish between one's personal style and their local business culture. Both are important. When you walk into that meeting you want to analyze and understand the person you are dealing with as an individual. What is their personal style? How do they conduct their business? You also want to understand the framework of the culture you are dealing with. How are meetings handled? Who is the decision maker? What can I do not to offend anyone?

Measure the person first. Apply the local standards second. And in doing so hopefully you will gain a new foreign partner and new foreign funding.

What follows are very broad based and generalistic statements about various facets of doing business in select countries. In an era of heightened sensitivities to anything that can be considered a stereotype or a value judgment what follows just might bother some readers. (Again, feel free to skip ahead to Chapter 16.)

Please know that it is not our intent to offend. It is our intent, however, to fully fund. You. In your business. (You've stuck with the book this far, thank you very much. Let's get your start up started.) If you can appreciate cultural differences, if you can develop strong personal relationships with business people around the world it seems to me that everyone is better off. There is better communication and understanding across the borders, unintentional offenses are avoided, deals get funded, people are employed, and wealth is created. It is all good.

Obviously, there is not space to include every country and every situation. If we did not include a country of interest that means you are going to have to obtain your own information. And even if we did briefly mention a country of interest you are still going to have to do your research. There is much to know and we want you to succeed. Understand and appreciate all the local customs by reading and consulting with your professionals in the host country. Your lawyers, accountants and other advisors can be of great assistance. As well, there are companies that offer courses in cross cultural awareness. If paying for a course allows you to build trust and better relationships with foreign partners it may be money well spent.

Again, what follows are generalizations. They will not necessarily apply to the individual you are dealing with or the situation you are in. Over time, as more and more people come into contact, some of these conditions may change. Please take them for what they are: General guideposts and not specific trail indicators.

And, as mentioned, by reading these scenarios you may learn a strategy that works for you wherever you are. Use it to your advantage.

We will first discuss meeting strategies, then a few unique business plan cases, then negotiations and finish with business cards. (When doing a business plan you can't forget to budget for good quality business cards.)

Meetings

The style and tenor of meetings can and will vary from country to country. Here are some examples of what to expect:

Australia

Meetings are relaxed but serious. Aussies prefer those who are modest and downplay their own successes. A good sense of humor, including self deprecating humor, is appreciated. Do not engage in high pressure sales tactics. Do expect to hear some colorful language.

Croatia

Meetings will be concluded when the meeting is done, and not when a certain time is reached. If you are traveling to Croatia keep your schedule flexible. Meetings can take on a life of their own.

Estonia

One of my clients is the type of person who fills a room, both literally and figuratively. He is a big man, with a booming voice, wild hand gestures and a knack for interrupting another with his latest, greatest thought. This is not how to do a business meeting in Estonia. Soft voices, minimal gesturing and a lack of conversation overlap are the norm. My client fortunately met with a savvy lawyer in Tallinn, Estonia's capital, before the meeting. With coaching the big bear became polite and contrite. He was always a man of his word. By taking it down a notch, and remaining reliable, he was able to fund his Estonian deal.

France

It is imperative to schedule an appointment for a meeting, which should be made at least two weeks in advance. July and August are tough times to get in to see someone as many are on vacation. If you don't speak French make an apology for not knowing the language. As well, knowing a few key French phrases will aid in developing a positive relationship. Avoid making excessive claims about your business plan. Exaggerations are not appreciated.

India

If you are traveling to India to present your business plan it is best to arrange for an appointment one to two months in advance. Be sure to reconfirm your appointment the week before and the day before the meeting. Meetings can be cancelled and rescheduled so keep your schedule open. Always arrive on time. Punctuality is important. Meetings initially involve small talk and getting acquainted chatter. Be prepared for the fact that little business may get done in the first meeting. Focus on getting to know your Indian hosts.

Ireland

Business meetings may occur in a restaurant or a pub, allowing everyone to be on an equal footing. Even in a pub setting, however, be careful not to be too loud or too full of yourself. The Irish are generally excellent conversationalists and enjoy verbal banter. They like to look at a business plan from all angles. Bring your A game and make a deal.

Italy

Appointments are a must and should be made in writing 2 to 3 weeks in advance. Reconfirm the meeting by telephone or fax. Don't even think about scheduling a meeting in August. Your business contemporaries are on vacation. Dressing well is imperative in Italy. Conservative suits for men and conservative dresses for women are favored for business meetings. Expensive accessories are acceptable for both women and men.

Malaysia

When asked a question you do not have to immediately respond. In fact, the Western style of quickly responding so as to show that you have not only mastered every detail but that you have them on the tip of your tongue may be considered rude by some in Malaysia. Pausing and giving thought to the question and then calmly responding is the preferred method in such gatherings. Of course, thinking before you speak is generally a good idea everywhere.

New Zealand

With people they don't know, New Zealanders can be pretty reserved. At the start, it is best if you are not too forward either. But once a relationship develops Kiwis can be surprisingly friendly and outgoing. They certainly appreciate a good sense of humor. In meetings it is important to be clear and direct. Your business plan and your presentation should state your proposals in a crisp and understandable fashion. Don't jump from pillar to post when speaking. By sticking to your points in a logical progression of thought you will be well received.

Poland

Be ready to engage in small talk. It is part of the relationship building process. Use any lunch or dinner meetings to forge a personal connection with your Polish colleagues. Once you have established that personal report meetings may become somewhat relaxed. However, the Polish participant with the most seniority will generally always open the meeting and set the agenda.

Portugal

The use of titles is important in Portugal. If one has a university degree they may be referred to as 'doutour' or 'doutoura' ("doctor") with or without their surname. Wait until you are permitted to operate on a first name basis. Similarly, continue using the formal case for the spoken word until your Portuguese colleague signals that informal speech is acceptable.

Sweden

Be on time for your meeting. Being late reflects very poorly on you. Thus, you may want to arrive a bit early to ensure you are punctual. Small talk is small at the start of a meeting. Although there can be exceptions, you will generally get right down to business. Be prepared to discuss the details of your business plan. Have any back up information and data handy as you may be called upon to discuss it.

Turkey

Turks prefer to do business with those they trust and personally like. They will want to engage with persons who are interested in a long relationship. So building a positive relationship is very important. Many first meetings are exclusively about getting to know each other. Only after a relationship is established will you be getting down to business.

U.S.A.

Do not expect a lot of small talk at the start of a meeting. Scheduling several busy people into one meeting may take some effort. Getting down to business is important as time is valuable. While the participants in a meeting may seem relaxed, the time and effort of a meeting is taken quite seriously. If you make a presentation, be direct. Visual aids are frequently used. Be sure to back up any claims as Americans like data and research.

At the end of the meeting there will be a summary of what was decided, what the next steps are and who will implement them.

Business Plan Particulars

In our research, we have come across three countries where business plans are required or have unique requirements.

Germany

A business plan can be considered mandatory in Germany. When starting a business in Germany there are a number of bureaucratic hurdles to overcome. You will need to register the business at the local court. You will then need to complete two tax registrations, one for the commercial tax and one at the local tax office. After these filings are complete, you can obtain a certificate of registration to commence business. Along the way, you will be talking to banks and applying for benefits with German authorities. In these discussions it is mandatory to have a business plan. Start writing. As well, in order to obtain permission to live and start a business in Germany several things are required including an application for a residence permit and a business plan. You really don't want to have to go through it all more than once.

Peru

A business plan can be considered almost mandatory in Peru. Starting a business in Peru means registering with the local government body. It is strongly suggested that you show adequate capital in a Peruvian bank account and a sound business plan as you proceed through this process.

South Africa

Business plans are crucial in South Africa for new businesses and existing businesses looking to expand. Any banker or investor will require a business plan. A unique element found in many South African business plans is a business continuity plan. This is a discussion of the priorities and strategies in the event of a system failure or disaster. Expect to be asked to see this additional section.

Negotiations

Your business plan will involve negotiations over ownership and funding. Work with a good negotiating team on your side, and appreciate the customs on the other side.

Argentina

If patience is a virtue, prepare to be virtuous.

Brazil

As is true in most countries, if you are not fluent in Portuguese, the language of Brazil, you are best served by hiring an experienced translator. It is best to use local accountants and lawyers as Brazilians may resent the presence of non-resident professionals. Your hosts negotiate with people not companies. Changing your negotiating team may result in having to restart negotiations from the beginning. As decisions are made by the highest ranking person be sure to understand the hierarchy in the room.

Canada

Being from a big country with plenty of room, Canadians like their own personal space. Speaking is done at arm's length and personal information is not readily forthcoming. Meetings begin with a minimal amount of small talk before getting down to business. Meetings with French speaking Canadians will be more hierarchical and will center on the most senior attendees. Meetings with English speaking Canadians may be more open with all parties contributing. When presenting your business plan be certain to be able to back up your claims with research and supporting information. Canadians are not given to exaggerated claims, and are suspicious of that which appears to be too good to be true.

China

Your business plan should be printed in both Chinese and your home language. During negotiations it is best if only the most senior member of your team speaks. (Please remember that when presenting your business plan.) Do not expect any decisions coming directly from the meetings you attend. Know that negotiations may occur at a very slow pace.

Ecuador

Ecuadorians want to know who they are doing business with. They may ask what some would consider intrusive questions so as to gauge your trust worthiness and reliability. While you may not want to reveal such information, an Ecuadorian may find your distance to be rude. At the same time, Ecuadorians speak with great courtesy and consider blunt communication also to be rude. So good luck with that conundrum. In your negotiations avoid confrontations and do not put others in an awkward position. Trust is paramount. If you agree to do something you had best follow through which, of course, is a good policy to follow anywhere around the world.

Japan

As many are aware, saving face is very important within Japanese society. Turning down someone's request results in embarrassment and a loss of face to the other person. Which, when negotiating a business deal, can be tricky. The whole idea is to get someone with money to accept your request for funding, or, in other words, to say "yes". If your request is something that cannot be agreed to look for a response akin to "it is under consideration" or "it is currently inconvenient." The party you are dealing with is saying no in a way that allows you to save face, which is actually quite thoughtful of them. Face equates to dignity and saving it is a good thing. But it can be frustrating for an outsider who has their future on the line to hear that their business plan is under consideration. In many cultures while that doesn't mean "yes" it also doesn't mean "no". In a related negotiation strategy, using a Japanese lawyer is viewed as a matter of goodwill. Your Japanese lawyer will also be able to tell you when "maybe" really means "no", thus saving you a great deal of wasted time and frustration.

Kenya

Kenyans are very diplomatic in newer and more formal relationships. Like the Japanese, maintaining honor and the avoidance of bringing shame upon another are important. A direct speaking style is not always the best manner. A more nuanced approach will serve you better in negotiations.

Lithuania

Business moves slowly in Lithuania and your business colleagues there will not be hurried into coming to an agreement. Each point will be discussed thoroughly before moving onto the next one. A deal will only be reached when the other side believes it is in their best interest to proceed. Be careful when dealing with time and deadlines. A client of mine hired a Lithuanian interpreter to assist in a business negotiation. When my client casually mentioned an impending deadline, the interpreter, being a good one, questioned my client first if he wanted to mention a time constraint. Not knowing the difference my client said to proceed. Once the issue of time was part of the mix the negotiations took a bad turn. In this case, the other side used time as a tactic and strung out the negotiations to their advantage. Even if time really is an issue, don't let it become one in your negotiations.

Mexico

Meeting face to face is important in Mexico, and be prepared for several meetings to be held before any sort of agreement is reached. Just like shopping in Mexico, expect some haggling. Never start with your best offer. This may entail preparing your business plan to provide for a lesser investment opportunity initially, which can be amended upwards when you reach a final agreement.

Netherlands

Expect very disciplined negotiations. Your Dutch counterparts will go through the smallest details. Communications will be very direct and frank. At the same time, negotiations can be as egalitarian as the culture. Everyone in the room is treated with respect. While it can take time to forge a contract, once it is signed a contract will be strictly enforced.

Russia

Be prepared for aggressive negotiations. Stay calm.

Slovakia

It is important to analyze the nature of the relationships when negotiating in Slovakia. For a new and/or formal relationship, there is an emphasis on diplomacy and finesse. Information will be delivered in a sensitive and cautious manner. As the parties become more acquainted, more direct and frank conversations will ensue. Relationships are very important. A huge amount of back up information for your business plan will be less important than the bond that needs to form. Meetings will come to a natural ending when the business is complete, and not according to a set time schedule.

South Korea

In South Korea contracts may be viewed more as memorandums of understanding. They can be considered as documents indicating a consensus to move forward with room for later adjustment and flexibility. Which to a Western trained attorney like me can be maddening. (The contract says X! You need to do X!) And which makes it all the more important to focus on developing a strong personal connection with your Korean counterpart. Use any meal or social event to establish mutual trust, respect and friendship. The best written contracts are always based on strong unwritten relationships.

Spain

Character and trust is important for Spanish investors. Face to face meetings are important. Expect your Spanish colleagues to be very thorough and detail oriented. Only after an oral agreement is reached will a written contract be prepared. Each side will be expected to adhere to the final contract.

Business Cards

No matter where you travel to present your business plan, be it across the globe or across the street, you will want to present you and your business in the best light possible. Investing in a high quality business card featuring your company logo on thick card stock is imperative. Do not ever give someone a card with tiny, serrated edges that you punched out after it was printed at home. You will not come off well, no matter what country you are in.

Chile

Business cards are presented at the very start of a meeting. In Chile, a creased or nicked business card will reflect very poorly on you. Actually, you should play the Chilean card – crisp, clean and smooth - around the world.

Indonesia

After the initial handshake business cards will be exchanged. Printing one side of your card in the Bahasa Indonesian language is a sign of respect. When giving and receiving cards, use two hands. This means you should not be holding other papers and materials at the start. Set them down and get ready to exchange. When receiving a business card, review it closely before putting it on the table for the meeting. Treat all business cards with respect.

Italy

Respect for one's business card is important in Italy. Look closely at it and read it before placing it away, ideally into a fancy business card case. Printing one side of your own card in Italian is always a good idea.

Japan

The exchanging of business cards is a ceremony in Japan. You must use only the highest quality cards and keep them in mint condition. Invest in a nice, conservative business card case to hold your cards and the flood of cards you are going to receive. If you are from outside Japan, have one side of your card printed in Japanese. Hand the Japanese side of the card to the recipient. You hand and receive business cards with two hands and a slight bow, as if you were dealing with an ounce of gold or other precious commodity. Because, in Japan, your business card is a precious commodity.

Philippines

Your business card should include your title and you should offer it first. Present and receive the card with two hands. Read the card before putting it into a business card case. Know that some senior executives will exchange their cards only to executives of similar rank.

Poland

Advanced degrees and titles are impressive on a business card in Poland. At the same time, cards are exchanged without a great deal of formality or ritual.

United Kingdom

With so much focus on the formality of business card exchanges in other countries, the usually protocol bound Brits may let you down on your exchange. Do not expect even a cursory glance before the card is shoved into their pocket. Do not be offended. It is not you.

Venezuela

At the start of a meeting during introductions business cards are exchanged with everyone at the meeting. So be sure to bring a sufficient number of cards. Have one side of the card printed in Spanish and present the recipient with the Spanish side up. On the card include all of your educational and professional qualifications as Venezuelans like knowing your status. Never write on someone's business card in front of them as it is viewed as extremely rude. Remember who the most senior person is in the room as you will want to send a thank you note after the meeting.

As we have gone through these cultural tips hopefully some of them may help you better your business success. Thinking before speaking as in Malaysia, being punctual for meetings as a sign of respect in India and Sweden, putting forth a quality business card as a reflection of yourselves in Chile and Japan are all excellent strategies no matter where you live. As well, civility and respect will go a long way in any country. Your business plan prospects will certainly benefit from the common wisdom of many cultures.

Chapter Sixteen

Business Plan Competitions

"Just do it."
– Nike

Win cash to start your own business!

It is almost like a dream come true. Which is why business plan competitions, where the winner gets start up money and free services to pursue their dream, have become more and more popular.

In a business plan competition you will submit your brilliantly drafted, expertly researched and graphically pleasing business plan (which, having read this book, you know how to do) to the contest organizer. The organizer may be a school or government agency or a non-profit organization. In some cases it may be a for profit company such as Tech Crunch or Intuit hosting a competition. As well, some competitions may focus on a market niche or business specialization such as green tech or social media.

In many contests it is a combination of both your written plan and an oral presentation that is judged. (Some thoughts on your final pitch will be discussed further down.)

The winners are generally decided by independent judges, many of whom are entrepreneurs and professionals involved with business start ups. As such, a significant benefit of entering your business plan into a contest is getting all sorts of free feedback from qualified people. So that if you don't initially win you may be able to use this valuable feedback to tweak, revise and rethink your plan to make it even better, thus allowing you to win with it later down the line.

Business plan competitions can offer some very meaningful cash prizes. While a majority are in the $5,000 to $25,000 range, the Accelerate Michigan Innovation Competition, for example, offers a $500,000 grand prize and a $150,000 runner up prize. To win you must either be a Michigan resident or agree to locate your company to Michigan. As the popularity of these competitions increase you can expect to see even higher cash prizes.

Joe Hurley is a CPA and the proprietor of www.bizplancompetitions.com, a leading web resource on business plan competitions. His website features a full calendar of competitions held throughout the U.S. and Canada.

Hurley has followed the rise of business plan competitions and attributes it to three factors. First, he says, there is a new focus on entrepreneurship. "There is a growing sense that encouraging the knowledge of how to start and run a business is a benefit to all." Combined with that is a desire to stimulate local and regional economies. Hurley states that: "Contests which encourage business formations and local hiring are seen, quite understandably, as a positive development for the community."

Finally, Hurley notes, there is a growing competition among business schools to have the best business plan competition. "A solid and prestigious competition," says Hurley "is now seen as a gauge of the quality of the school's overall program."

With business plan competitions competing to be the best business plan competition, everyone wins in the form of higher cash prizes and more opportunities to vet your ideas in front of feedback providing experts.

Business plan competitions are now also hosted around the world. From Canada to Thailand and to places in between, competitions are encouraging entrepreneurs to draft their plan and compete for their dream.

TechnoServe is a non profit corporation that helps entrepreneurs in developing countries start and expand business ventures. They are donor funded with 1,000 employees and 150 consultant volunteers in 25 countries.

TechnoServe has found that an excellent means to identify and assist promising entrepreneurs is to hold business plan competitions nationally and offer prizes of $10,000 to $25,000, along with continuing 'after care' services including accounting, legal and marketing expertise. Participants attend workshops to learn how to hone and refine their business ideas into workable plans.

Bruce McNamer is the head of TechnoServe and explains the benefits. "The competitions allow entrepreneurs to work with capital funding sources early on. By integrating the money side with the business plan training we are able to bridge a very real gap in developing countries between deals and funding."

A second benefit is getting the local business community involved. "When the banking, accounting, legal, marketing and other professional sectors become engaged with start up and expanding businesses," says McNamer, "you end up with a more robust business sector. It all builds the infrastructure for future successes."

It is important to realize that the returns may not be immediate. "We are in a catalyst role," says McNamer. "This is something that must be invested in over time before any returns can be measured."

Still, the business plan competitions TechnoServe has held in fifteen countries throughout Africe, Latin and South America have been successful and transformative. "The business plan workshops and training help entrepreneurs shape their ideas into formal and structured plans. That process alone creates future winners."

For more information on TechnoServe's ongoing business plan competitions throughout the world visit www.TechnoServe.org.

A recent survey helps to underscore the benefits of such competitions. The Burton D. Morgan Business Plan Competition has been held at Purdue University since 1987. To understand how the competition has affected past finalists, Purdue's Krannert School of Management conducted a survey. The results were impressive:

- 86% of the respondents said participating in the competition enhanced their education.

- 67% said they now viewed themselves as entrepreneurs.

- 59% said the competition influenced their career goals.

- 35% said they started a company right after being a finalist

- 41% said they started a company later in their career.

Clearly, some positive results are emerging from business plan competitions.

I have served as a judge in the Governor's Cup Business Plan Competition, which is run by Dave Archer and open to all college students throughout the state of Nevada. After reading ten business plans, the judges panel listened to ten oral presentations. Of course, some presentations were better than others. Wanting to know why, I interviewed the finalists. The difference came down to one word: Practice.

Why someone wouldn't practice their presentation was, at least initially, beyond me. But some felt so overwhelmed with getting the written part right that they said they didn't have time to perfect the oral part. Others were more or less along for the ride. That is, they wanted the experience but didn't really want to start a company just yet. They weren't going to give it their all. Not nailing the presentation was their way, in horse racing terms, of pulling back on the reins so that their horse didn't win.

In a similar vein, some had come to learn through the whole time consuming preparation process that they really did not want to start a business with their current partners. Winning and moving forward with people you do not, can not, and never will get along with is not a good idea. If the business plan competition teaches you that starting a business is like getting married, and that you'd better be able to get along with your partners through some challenging times, you will have learned a hugely valuable lesson. Not winning the competition so that you avoid the stress of an unworkable partnership is, in a sense, winning.

Conversely, those who really wanted to win practiced their oral presentation. They practiced it many times in front of various people who were encouraged to offer blunt but constructive criticism. You cannot practice in a vacuum. Not only does nature abhor it but you will never get any better without critical minds offering feedback and pushback on all your points with the goal of making you and your presentation better. And so the winners of the competition were those who had both a winning business plan and a winning oral presentation.

A strategy (or shall we say 'a trick') I have seen business plan judges use is to engage the competitors to give them their elevator pitch on the plan. By hearing a short, focused business explanation, judges (and all sorts of potential investors) can get to the heart of the matter quickly. And so it is important for you to develop your elevator pitch.

Melvin and Seglinda

Melvin had developed his business plan and was going downtown to see his accountant about the final draft. The office building his accountant used was also the home to a number of investment bankers and venture capitalists.

Melvin got on the elevator with Seglinda, an attractive, professionally dressed woman in her 40's. She could see that Melvin was carrying a business plan and asked what type of venture Melvin as looking to start.

Melvin was brilliant. In 45 seconds, using clear and powerful language, he told the story of a compelling problem that his business plan would solve. He laid out a hook and Seglinda rose to the bait. As she got off the elevator she said she wanted to know more. Melvin said he would stop by after meeting with his accountant.

As Melvin was meeting with the CPA he casually mentioned that a lady named Seglinda down on the 40th floor wanted to meet him when they were done. The CPA was impressed. Seglinda was one of the top venture people at her prestigious venture capital firm.

Melvin went to visit Seglinda after finishing up with his CPA. She had approved of his elevator pitch and liked his well thought out and clearly drafted business plan even better. Melvin was soon funded

As Melvin's case demonstrates, having a clear and concise pitch that you could make while travelling in the proverbial short elevator ride is imperative. You never know when someone will ask for the thumbnail version of your one hundred page business plan. But you can bet they will ask. People have less and less time. Their attention spans are short. You need to grab them with your pitch to get them to move onto your business plan.

So, what are the elements of a great elevator pitch?

1. Your story. There is a very real problem that is either solved or bad things result. Your business plan solves the problem. Tell that story.

2. Powerful and visual. Use powerful words to create a visual image in your listener's head. Play to the theater of the mind.

3. Clear. While your words are powerful they are not fancy. Use clear wording that everyone understands. Stay away from industry jargon.

4. Your goal. Know exactly what outcome you want. Is it to read your plan, invest in your business or make a sale? Pitch to your goal.

5. The hook. Set the hook so that they want more. Remember, you've only got under a minute here. They're not going to be signing a check, at least not yet. The hook strikes a chord, and has them exchanging business cards with you for more.

6. Practice, practice, practice.

You and your team will spend more time crafting a short pitch that you will ever imagine. As Mark Twain famously said: "If I had more time I would have written a shorter letter."

You will start big with your story, your goals, and the action statements associated with your goals. Write it all down. Sleep on it. Let it sit for a day. Come back to it again and again. Prepare a five minute pitch (which may be useful to have for certain business plan competitions). You may want to experiment with several styles of longer pitches, conservative, funny, etc. Rehearse the longer pitch and record it. Come back to it and see which phrases are clear and powerful. Understand which phrases hook the listener. Weed out the extraneous. Continue to practice, rehearse and record. Continue to narrow it down. Experiment with several variations of the new shorter pitch. Any words or phrases that do not lead you to your goal should be removed. You are going from Tolstoy to Hemingway. Your words are sparse but vivid.

Do a dress rehearsal. Present one or more pitches to friends, family and colleagues. Get their feedback. Gauge what interests them. Continue to refine. You are going from just another slab of rock to your own finely cut and polished diamond.

Record the final pitch. Set it aside for a few days. When you come back to it ask: Is this the best we can do?

If not, keep working on it. If it is, remember to keep polishing and cutting your diamond. As your business and goals change, so does your pitch. It will never be static. It will always be improving.

The elevator pitch has become such an important part of the business funding process that schools now offer courses on it. In fact, as a subset of business plan competitions, Duke University's Fuqua School of Business now holds an elevator pitch competition. You've got one minute to win it.

Chapter Seventeen

Conclusion

"A purpose is the eternal condition of success"
– Theodore T. Munger

Remember that your business plan is a plan. It reflects your purpose and identity. It is your roadmap and guide. It is remarkably easy to get so caught up in the numbers and the search for funding that you forget that your plan can actually improve your business. Whether your plan is for an existing business or for a startup, whatever stage your business happens to be in, use your business plan to both stick to your purpose and to anticipate and address potential problems before they ever arise.

The key to using your plan as a true planning document (as opposed to just part of a loan application) is to actually *use* the plan. Don't just finish it up and stick it in a drawer. A business plan, at its best, is a constantly evolving, organic document that changes with your business. Use it to help you win.

Keep a handle on all aspects of your business plan and thus your business. Watch to see if your plans are helping your bottom line. Keep analyzing your business and your plans for the future.

Remember all those financial projections you made? They weren't just to impress potential funders and investors. They are goals for your business, and you need to come back to them periodically (monthly is reasonable) to see how you are doing at meeting your goals. Be prepared to adjust those goals as you go along. As your business abilities improve, so will your goal-setting abilities. Every month you should get better at analyzing future potential by current costs and revenues. Keep projections realistic by keeping them current.

Most business problems creep up on business owners in small increments. By checking in with your plan on a monthly basis, you can see problems when they are still small. Is your advertising plan doing what you had hoped? Are sales increasing? If not, why? It's much better to start making changes when sales are down a few hundred dollars than when they are down several thousands. Your business plan is a road map for your business, checking in will help you keep on course.

Don't just concentrate on the marketing and finances, the schemes and the numbers. Periodically, come back to your vision and goals. Remember why you got into business and what you wanted to gain, in addition to money. Always be ready to ask yourself if you are where you want to be and if your business is what you want it to be.

Consult your timelines and keep them current. There are very few timelines that are initially accurate. The deeper you get into a project, especially one as complicated as expanding or starting a business, the more holes you will find in your timeline.

Preparing your business plan is an excellent way for you to identify all the steps it will take to make your business a success. But that preparation will also show you how many contingencies you have virtually no control over. For example, loans may not come through as quickly as planned or you may have to move more quickly than you had planned in order to get the property you want. Legislation may throw a political wrench into your plans. Intellectual property (yours or someone else's) may make or break your company. And then there's luck, which we have no real control over either.

But following the steps herein, by creating your winning business plan, you can lure luck into your corner. Opportunity is where luck meets preparation. And by preparing a winning business plan all opportunities will be open to you. Good Luck.

Appendix A

Business Startup Check List

Start Planning for Success

- Describe your business concept

- Describe your business values (how your business will impact others such as employees, customers, the environment). This helps to develop your company culture. For example, Walt Disney created "The Disney Spirit" and each year cast members can be nominated by their peers to receive the Disney Spirit Award.

- Research your market

- Identify your target market

- Research your competitors and suppliers

- Identify your strategic position

- Consider potential exit strategy's

- Identify your business entity structure

- Identify your management team

- Create a business plan

- Create a marketing plan

- Create a funding plan based off of your business plan financials.

Create Your Company Brand

- Choosing business name
- Obtain trademarks
- Create logos, and colors
- Create taglines
- Create business cards and letterhead
- Obtain a domain name
- Create a business website & email address (having a business email address helps to create a professional image for your company and speaks to the level of business sophistication of business owners. It also helps you to build business credit.)

Getting through the Red Tape

- Business entity formation (Corporation , LLC, etc.)
- Qualify your company to conduct business in the state you are physically located in unless it's the same state your company business entity was filed in
- Setup your physical location (Residential or Commercial)
- Obtain a TIN
- Select Your Standard Industrial Classification Number (SIC)
- Select Your North American Industry Classification System Number (NAICS)
- Obtain all state and local licenses such as business license and resale permits
- Obtain phone number that can be listed in 411 directories (Usually a land line)
- Obtain a Fax number
- Open a business bank account (do not co-mingle your personal funds and your business funds)
- Obtain business insurance/bonding as needed.

Prepare a Financial Foundation

- Meet with an accountant
- Learn about tax rights and responsibilities (www.irsvideos.gov/SmallBusinessTaxpayer)
- Learn finance/accounting terminology
- Pull your personal credit reports and clean up any credit issues
- Setup your bookkeeping
- Build business credit (www.BusinessCreditSuccess.com)
- Setup terms with your vendors/suppliers
- Setup a merchant account to accept credit cards.

Appendix B

Business Plan for Mikhail's Tacos, Inc.

Mikhail's Tacos, Inc.
4428 College Street
Reno, NV 89503
Mikhail Ramnikov, President
February 1, 20__

Table of Contents

I. Mission Statement
II. Executive Summary
III. The Business
- Strengths and Weaknesses
- Legal Structure
- Business Description
- Product Description
- Intellectual Property Description
- Location
- Management and Personnel
- Records
- Insurance
- Security
- Litigation
IV. Marketing
- Markets
- Competition
- Distribution and Sales
- Industry and Market Trends
- Industry Assessment
- Marketing Strategies
- Customer Service
V. Financials
- Uses of Funds
- Income Statement
- Cash Flow Statement
- Balance Sheet
- Income Projection
- Break-Even Analysis
VI. Supporting Documents

I. Mission Statement

The mission of Mikhail's Tacos, Inc. is to sell flavorful and unique gourmet Mexican food in a pleasing dining atmosphere.

II. Executive Summary

Mikhail Ramnikov is the president of Mikhail's Tacos, Inc. He is an experienced businessman who also specializes in creative food preparation. His brother, Alexei Ramnikov, is an experienced chef. The brothers enjoy preparing unique gourmet Mexican food. Together, the two have contributed $50,000 in personal funds to advance the operations of the company.

Mikhail's Tacos, Inc. seeks to raise $50,000 from investors to commence operations. Investors will receive a priority return of their money back from first profits and upon repayment shall own 25% of the then issued stock in the company.

Mikhail's special recipes feature anything but the traditional ingredients and toppings. Creative flavors will set Mikhail's apart from its competitors. Mikhail's will cater to the built-in market of college students, business people, and affluent shoppers that frequent the area. Amid a sea of fast-food restaurants that populate this area, Mikhail's will offer its fresh, expertly prepared menu in a relaxed dining environment.

Significant market research and target market evaluation suggest that Mikhail's Tacos is ideally situated to cater to an unfulfilled market segment. Proven marketing techniques and operational systems will allow management to be proactive rather than reactive to the conditions and obstacles associated with opening a new restaurant concept.

Having a sound operational plan allows management to focus on building sales rather than profit. The managing partners have an extremely high degree of confidence that the systems and controls incorporated in the business plan will yield a calculated return for a given sales volume.

We feel the business plan for Mikhail's Tacos represents a realistic expectation of success for all parties involved. Moreover, we will be providing a benefit to the community by providing a great product and secure jobs to community residents.

CONFIDENTIALITY STATEMENT: Information contained in this business plan is strictly confidential and is being presented to specific persons with the understanding that those persons will maintain confidentiality and not disclose or distribute any part of this plan to third parties without the prior written permission of the author(s). Information includes any data, reports, schedules, or attachments that may be contained in or referred to in this document.

III. The Business

Strengths and Weaknesses

Management believes that the strength of Mikhail's Tacos, Inc. is found in the fresh, quality ingredients used to prepare their uniquely flavored tacos, burritos, and other Mexican dishes. Mikhail's will provide creative alternatives to traditional Mexican food along with popular favorites – all for an affordable price in a comfortable setting.

The main weakness is the lack of brand recognition, as is common with most start-up businesses. Mikhail is a recent immigrant from Russia – and with his brother Alexei, prepares outstanding Mexican food from his own recipes. This amazing story, the likes of which could only take place in America, will separate Mikhail's from its competitors and lead to brand awareness.

Mikhail's can fill the niche of a creative and original locally owned hotspot, which is much desired in an area filled with chain restaurant clones.

Though Mikhail has never owned a food service business, he owned his own bicycle repair shop in Moscow for twelve years, managing every detail of the business successfully. Mikhail specializes in friendly, fast, and efficient customer service that will easily be carried over into the restaurant business. Alexei is a chef with over twenty years experience in the restaurant business.

Legal Structure

Mikhail's Tacos, Inc. is organized as a Nevada corporation. It has elected S Corporation status and is taxed as a flow-through entity. Mikhail Ramnikov is the president and Alexei Ramnikov is the secretary and treasurer of the company. Both serve on the Board of Directors.

Mikhail and Alexei Ramnikov's previous business experience can be found under the section titled "Management and Personnel."

Business Description

Mikhail's Tacos will sell gourmet tacos in a rented existing retail space on College Street, located equidistantly between the University of Nevada, Reno campus and a nearby stable business district. The food will be prepared quickly, but will not be fast food. Mikhail's will provide fresh, healthy food in a relaxed, sit-down environment.

The restaurant will include indoor and outdoor patio seating areas as well as a bar. All food will be prepared on site from ingredients purchased from a team of suppliers. The establishment will be open Sunday through Thursday, serving lunch and dinner from 11:00 a.m. until 9:00 p.m. On Friday and Saturday, Mikhail's will be open from 11:00 a.m. until 11:00 p.m.

The restaurant décor will combine traditional Mexican elements with American surf culture and the music will be a blend of Mexican and American pop tunes. Every spot in the restaurant will remain clean, which is both pleasing to the customer and in keeping with Mikhail's fastidious nature.

A sample menu is found on the next page.

Mikhails's Tacos Menu

Appetizers

Homemade chips and salsa..2.25

Homemade chips and guacamole...4.75

Super Nachos "the works" with charbroiled chicken and black beans.......8.25

Nachos chips with melted cheeses, sour cream, guacamole and salsa........5.75

Add Chicken....add 3.00   Add Steak....add 3.75   Add Fish....4.00

Coconut Crunchy Shrimp four prawns rolled in sweet coconut, fried and served

with orange chili dipping sauce..8.95

Quesadilla grilled flour tortilla folded with melted cheeses...........................4.00

Add Sautéed Veggies...add 3.00   Add Chicken.................................add 3.00

Add Steak................add 3.75   Add Shrimp or Acapulco Shrimp...add 4.00

Add Fish..................add 4.00   Add Del Mar/Salmon Fish.............add 5.00

Brie & Mango Salsa Quesadilla sweet & savory taste treat...........................6.95

Steak Ranchero Taquitos hot & spicy steak rolled in crispy corn tortilla.........7.00

Chicken Mango Flautas chicken & mango salsa rolled in crispy flour tortilla......7.00

Warm flour tortillas (3) with citrus honey butter.................................1.00

Homemade, vegetarian pinto beans, black beans or rice....................2.25

Soups and Salads

Chicken-Lime Tortilla Soup homemade comfort soup............................4.50

Caesar Salad Tijuana classic with romaine, parmesan and tortilla strips.........5.75

Tostada Salad flour tortilla shell topped with beans, lettuce, cheese and sals........5.75

Mexicana Salad flour tortilla shell filled with mixed greens, topped with carrots, beets,

garbanzo beans, pumpkin seeds and queso fresco, with homemade dress.................5.75

To any of the above salads: Add Chicken.....................................add 3.00

Add Steak.............add 3.75   Add Shrimp or Acapulco Shrimp......add 4.00

Add Fish...............add 4.00   Add Del Mar/Salmon Fish................add 5.00

Specialties

All Specialties served with choice of beans, rice and warm flour tortilla

Coconut Crunchy Shrimp seven prawns rolled in sweet coconut, fried and served with orange chili dipping sauce..14.95

Fresh Fish charbroiled and served with mango salsa (see board for today's fish)....12.95

Chicken Breast spice-rubbed and charbroiled with mango salsa....................10.95

Steak marinated and charbroiled served with Pico de Gallo salsa.....................12.50

Fajitas-Steak, Chicken, or Shrimp served with sautéed vegetables at above prices

Coconut Crunchy Tofu vegetarian delight with orange chili dipping sauce....9.95

Enchiladas choose from chicken or shrimp with chipotle or verde salsa..............9.25

Shashlyk Mikhail's specialty. Traditional Russian marinated pork grilled on a skewer with onions and served with spicy sour cream sauce.....................................14.95

Tacos and Burritos

Guacamole, sour cream, cheese and mango salsa upon request.
All Tacos served with cabbage slaw, on corn tortillas, or flour tortilla upon request. All Burritos served with rice and choice of beans wrapped in flour tortilla. Burritos may be ordered on a whole wheat tortilla or may be ordered "wet" with salsa and cheese melted on top

taco / burrito

Chicken spice rubbed and charbroiled with Pico de Gallo salsa.........4.50/7.25

Chicken Verde chicken stewing in salsa verde............................4.50/7.25

Buenos charbroiled fish with mango salsa and citrus honey butter............4.95/7.95

Baja San Felipe-style fried fish with sour cream chili sauce....................5.25/8.60

Shrimp sautéed shrimp with garlic butter....................................4.85/7.95

Acapulco Shrimp as above with tomatoes, onions, cilantro, parmesan......4.95/8.00

Steak marinated and charbroiled with Pico de Gallo salsa.........................4.85/7.75

Steak Ranchero marinated spicy carne asada...............................4.85/7.75

Vegetarian vegetables sautéed in marinade with citrus honey butter..........4.50/7.25

Tofu spice rubbed tofu, red pepper with citrus honey butter....................4.50/7.25

Coconut Crunchy Tofu rolled in coconut flakes, with orange chili sauce...4.50/7.25

International Wraps

All International Wraps are served wrapped in a flour tortilla

Chicken Caesar Wrap crisp Caesar salad with charbroiled chicken and rice......7.75
Cajun Jambalaya Wrap shrimp, spicy sausage and Cajun seasoned rice............7.95
Del Mar Caesar Wrap crisp Caesar salad with spice-rubbed salmon and rice...8.60
Chicken Ranch Wrap crispy chicken, lettuce and ranch dressing....................6.95
St. Petersburg Fish Wrap crispy trout, crunchy cabbage, dill and spicy sour cream
sauce...8.95

Children's Plates

Baja Fish Taco fried fish with cabbage slaw wrapped in flour tortilla................4.75
Cheese Quesadilla flour tortilla folded with melted cheeses...........................2.95
Bean and Cheese Burrito in flour tortilla...3.25
Chicken and Cheese Wrap in a flour tortilla..4.15
Crispy Chicken Strips with ketchup or ranch...3.75
Pinto beans, black beans or Mexican rice..2.25
Charbroiled Chicken served in a bowl...3.00

Salsa Bar

Enjoy any of our five freshly made salsas on the salsa bar.

Twelve ounce salsa-to-go container with chips....................................3.50
Homemade chips and salsa...2.25

Desserts

Mexican Flan sweet cinnamon custard..3.00
Apple Changa apples in a crispy tortilla w/ vanilla ice cream........................5.00
Churros two Mexican donuts rolled in cinnamon sugar................................2.25

Beverages

Tequila Margarita frozen or on the rocks..4.75

Pint Margarita....................7.50   Pitcher Margarita............................15.25

100% Agave "sipping" Tequilas...............(please see server for selection and price)

Beer/Cerveza Domestic....3.25   Mexican Beer..................................3.50

Micro-brew/Non Alcoholic   in bottle....3.50   on tap.........4.25

Wine, by the glass/bottle (please see selection & prices at register)

Homemade Red Wine Sangria   glass...........4.00   carafe.........12.00

Hibiscus Flower Iced Tea or Lemonade (free refills)...............................1.85

Vitamin Water (available in assorted flavors)...2.65

Bottled Water/Orange Juice/Milk..1.85

Horchata cinnamon rice drink..1.85

Jarritos (strawberry, orange, grapefruit flavored soda)..1.85

Freshly Brewed Latin Coffee/Hot Tea...1.85

Coke/Diet Coke/Sprite/Root Beer, etc (free refills)..............................1.85

Mikhail's Tacos gift certificates & logo wear

The Perfect Gift! Mikhail's T-shirt..14.95

Mikhail's gift certificates are available in any denomination

Join us for Happy Hour! Daily 3:30 – 6:00 p.m.
Casual Catering available for your parties

After the brand and product have become easily recognized and popular, the company will consider expanding to one or more additional locations within three years of opening the original restaurant. Another goal is to establish Mikhail's as a catering option for events held around town. This service will further establish the brand identity among locals.

Product Description

Mikhail's will prepare made-to-order gourmet tacos with only the finest and freshest ingredients available. Mikhail's recipes use unique flavors to enhance tacos and burritos, including mango salsas and margarita-marinated mahi mahi. Traditional Mexican fare will be offered as well.

The bar will specialize in fruit-infused margaritas, but will also carry a variety of imported Mexican tequilas and Russian vodkas. A selection of beers will be available as well.

Fresh ingredients will be purchased from local suppliers. All tortillas will be hand-made on site by a team of two food preparation specialists expertly trained by Mikhail and his brother, Alexei. The kitchen staff will prepare all food made-to-order, meaning that customers can add or leave out ingredients as they choose.

Although the restaurant is designed to offer a sit-down environment, it is expected that most patrons will want their food quickly since they will be students eating between classes and business people stopping in during their lunch breaks. Take-out orders will always be available. While a delivery service will not be offered immediately, this could be added if there is a demand.

Intellectual Property Description

The company has obtained the domain name www.mikhailstacos.com and has applied for a federal trademark registration of the name Mikhail's Tacos. All company recipes shall be treated as trade secrets until the company decides, in its sole discretion, to publish a cookbook of selected recipes.

Location

Mikhail's location, at the corner of State and College streets, was chosen because of its proximity to two major customer bases. To date, there are few inexpensive restaurants near the University of Nevada, Reno campus, which has an enrollment of 20,000 students, and is projected to grow to 30,000 students in the next eight years. The restaurant's proposed location will be within walking distance for easy student access. Mikhail's is equally close to a stable business and shopping district. This area is overloaded with unhealthy, fast food options, but is lacking a healthy, sit-down alternative.

This is a high-traffic, high-visibility location. These two streets are the main thoroughfares for students commuting to class as well as business people and shoppers accessing the nearby mall and surrounding businesses. It is within walking distance of the university's football and basketball venues. It is likely that Wolf Pack game days will attract a large crowd of customers.

It is expected that there may be a seasonal lapse in business from the college students during the summer months when a more limited summer session is held. However, customers from surrounding businesses and hungry shoppers will not have an "off season" and their business may even increase during popular shopping periods, such as December.

This location previously housed a pizzeria. (The pizza business closed due to the sudden death of the owner and not from a lack of business.) Many of the kitchen appliances (such as refrigeration units, ovens, and microwaves) are already in place. A new hood will have to be purchased for the kitchen. Remodeling is planned for the dining room area. A bar must be installed, as well as new tables and booths to allow for more seating. The original wood flooring will be used, but new paint, moldings, and countertops will be added. The bathrooms are not in good condition and will have to be completely redone. A new brightly lit sign for both the exterior of the building and the shopping center marquis will be purchased and installed.

A computerized ordering system will be installed to ease in the ordering process. This system will also perform payment functions, such as credit card sales. This will assist the company with its record keeping. (See "Records" Section.)

There is adequate, well-lit parking available for customers and staff. Night patrons will have additional parking since many of the businesses in the shopping center will be closed in the evening.

Management and Personnel

Mikhail Ramnikov, President of Mikhail's Tacos, Inc. has had extensive business experience in Moscow before his move to the United States. He started up his own bicycle repair and supply shop and ran it successfully for over ten years. Although his experience has not been in the restaurant business, he has successfully marketed and managed a business from the ground up in the past. He will also serve on the Board of Directors for the corporation.

Alexei Ramnikov was trained as a chef in Moscow over twenty years ago. He worked at a successful hotel restaurant in Moscow as the head chef for 15 years before moving to Los Angeles five years ago. There he worked as head chef in a gourmet bistro until his move to Reno, NV. He is the secretary and treasurer of Mikhail's Tacos, Inc. and will serve on the Board of Directors.

Mikhail's will require food servers, busboys, kitchen staff, a dishwasher, a bartender, and a host/hostess. Mikhail himself will bartend and greet customers initially, with plans to hire additional help for these positions as business increases. Waiters and waitresses will be recruited from the student population. The dining room will only require two waiters per shift. However, when hiring students, hours and schedules will have to be flexible. Therefore, a staff of eight waiters and waitresses will be hired initially to rotate and cover shifts as their school schedules allow. Two busboys will be hired, but only one will work per shift. Mikhail will train all wait-staff as they are hired. The day will be broken into two shifts for food servers, one for lunch and one for dinner.

Mikhail's brother, Alexei, is the trained cook with over ten years of restaurant experience. He will oversee the kitchen and will train his staff as they are hired. A staff of four food preparation experts and two dishwashers will be hired to assist Alexei. Only two cooks will work in the kitchen at all times. Additionally, Alexei will supervise most shifts and order ingredients from suppliers as needed.

Mikhail will be in charge of records and bookkeeping, including payroll. An attorney and accountant will be hired to advise Mikhail and Alexei on necessary matters.

Records

Mikhail is proficient in both record keeping and bookkeeping because of his previous business experience. At his bicycle shop, Mikhail handled both duties successfully. Initially, Mikhail will perform these functions. After two months, an outside bookkeeper will be hired. All records will be carefully kept at both the home office and the restaurant office. Employee files will be kept in a locked file cabinet and employees will not have access to the files.

Management will practice sound management procedures in order to control costs, insure quality of product and provide friendly customer service. The following systems will be used by management:

Point of Sale (POS) System

Careful evaluation and dutiful research will be used in the selection of a POS (point of sale) system that best meets the needs of Mikhail's Tacos. The POS system will be configured with requisition printing, a process which forces food and beverage items to be registered in the system before the items can be prepared. Requisition printing has proven to reduce costs by as much as 3-5%. The POS system will also be the control center to regulate the flow of service and item preparation. Built-in cash controls will help in tracking sales and receipts.

Cash Audits

Management will conduct periodic cash audits for all cashier stations. Surprise shift audits are an effective tool to determine cashier/bartender under ringing.

Scheduling System

Management will adopt a scheduling system that expedites the preparation of schedules, reflects anticipated labor budgets, and helps to regulate labor costs.

Operations Checklists

The restaurant will be managed with the use of various checklists. Consistent use of checklists will help to maintain quality control while ensuring that established procedures are followed. Checklists will be used by various personnel for customer service, purchasing, receiving and storage, preparation, cleaning, shift changes, opening and closings.

Order Guide

The restaurant will use an item specific order guide to track order history and maintain designated levels of product in inventory.

Weekly Inventory

Management will conduct a weekly inventory to determine valuation for use in the preparation of weekly profit and loss reports.

Video Surveillance

Video surveillance will be in place to monitor activities and deter crime.

Safety Reviews

Periodic safety assessments will be performed to ensure that employees and guests are not exposed to dangerous or harmful conditions or actions.

Liability Reviews

Periodic assessments will also be done to evaluate the liability exposure of the restaurant. Alcohol awareness, employee relations and guest treatment will be scrutinized from time to time.

Insurance

Insurance for the building will include public liability and property damage coverage. A worker's compensation plan will also be purchased. Employees working full-time (30 hours/week) will have the option of being on the restaurant's health plan. The hour requirement will most likely limit the employees using this plan to Mikhail, Alexei, and the kitchen and busing staff. It is expected that the servers will be students working limited amounts of hours.

Security

The key security risks involved with the restaurant include stolen money and equipment. To combat these risks, an alarm system will be installed and will be activated during non-business hours. Only Mikhail and Alexei will have keys to the building and to the file cabinets containing personal information. No money will be left in the restaurant overnight. Mikhail or Alexei will remove all money earned during the day before leaving.

A computer system will be installed not only to ease in the ordering process, but also to keep track of what is being ordered and how it is being paid for. Mikhail will tend to most duties at the bar to eliminate the risk of having bar profits stolen.

Litigation

Neither the company nor Management are subject to any existing or threatened litigation.

IV. Marketing

Markets

Mikhail's Tacos will be attractive to a variety of different markets. The first market it will appeal to is college students because of the low prices, fast preparation, and close proximity to campus. It also will appeal to nearby business people because they can get a quick and healthy lunch and still get back to the office on time. Weary shoppers will be attracted to the restaurant's sit-down design. It will be a fresh alternative to the fast food establishments that surround the mall. It will also appeal to families because of the friendly and relaxed atmosphere that accompanies the low prices.

Other markets the restaurant will cater to are health-conscious eaters and diners that prefer to frequent locally owned restaurants rather than chains. The take-out option will attract another set of customers that want quality food quickly.

While the city of Reno suffered in the Great Recession, the University continued to expand, bringing more jobs and students to the local market. It is anticipated that this trend will continue.

Competition

The restaurant's main competition will be with two chain restaurants that offer the same basic category of food: Taco Bell and Baja Fresh. Both have national brand recognition. The prices are lower for both competitors, but the food qualifies as fast food and is not of the same quality. Taco Bell has a location near the mall while Baja Fresh is located in a shopping center near campus. Both offer seating, but not a full-service restaurant. Mikhail's also offers a full bar, which neither of the competitors have. Mikhail's boasts the innovative use of gourmet ingredients, which will further separate them from the competition.

Other competitors include the variety of restaurants in the area, including Burger King, McDonald's, Pizza Hut, and a locally owned pub and sandwich shop. Mikhail's does have slightly higher prices, but they also offer a different product in a different environment. The product is still produced quickly as it is at these other restaurants. The fact that there is a dining room and bar encourages people to bring their friends and family to Mikhail's for an evening out, whereas you would most likely choose the other restaurants as strictly a fast dining option.

While many of these competitors are nationally recognized brands, Mikhail's can attract a following with the quality and creativity of the food, the low prices, and the service and friendly environment.

Distribution and Sales

Menu items will be offered both for dining-in, with casual service provided by the wait staff, and for take-out with patrons picking up their meals.

Pricing will range from $4.50 for traditional tacos to a spice rubbed fish burrito at $8.60. All menu items fall within this range except for certain specialty dishes, which will cost up to $14.95, depending on the type of ingredients featured. Certain meals will include rice and beans.

Bar items will include beers priced from $3.25-$4.25, and hard liquor drinks priced between $4.75 and $8.00, depending on the liquor called. Fresh fruit margaritas will sell at $4.75 for individuals and at $15.25 for pitchers. Prices for margaritas increase as top-shelf tequila is requested.

Industry and Market Trends

The identified markets in this area have many choices when it comes to eating out. However, most of these choices are limited to fast food options only. There are very few quality, dine-in restaurants in this area that offer affordable prices. Mikhail's will fill an in-between niche that has yet to be tapped. The restaurant is not a chain fast food restaurant, yet is not so upscale that it is too expensive or intimidating for the average diner.

Market research conducted informally by Mikhail and Alexei has shown that people in this neighborhood enjoy Mexican cuisine on the whole, but don't like the greasy and unhealthy nature of most of their nearby options. Many diners have also commented on the lack of locally owned and operated restaurants in the area. It seems that in this area, a trend to move away from chain restaurants has been identified.

Market research experts have also identified this trend nationally. Research has shown that only 2.6% of Americans ate at a fast-casual chain restaurant in the last week, leading to the assumption that there are a great number of diners wanting to explore fresh tastes and ideas by taking chances on unknown names and brands.

This research also shows that the market for fast and casual food has grown at a rate of 5.7% per year since 2009. This growth has been attributed to the quick preparation taken from fast-food restaurants combined with the comfort and ambience of restaurant dining. Most of these types of restaurants have also put an emphasis on freshness and health consciousness. Many of these types of chains do not also offer alcoholic beverages, thus limiting the market. However, Mikhail's Tacos, Inc. will fulfill this desire for customers.

Overall, more and more Americans are predicted to dine out this year. For example, national research shows that this year there will be an increase of over 8 billion meals and 7 billion snacks eaten out. Young adults are found to make up a large portion of restaurant users – which bodes well for Mikhail's Tacos since it is targeting college students. A recent survey showed that the number of full-service restaurants offering food for takeout is increasing rapidly, showing there is a demand for this type of service. One survey revealed that many Americans consider takeout essential for their lifestyles.

Industry Assessment

According to the National Restaurant Association, industry sales for 2011 are expected to rise above the $580 billion dollars spent on dine out meals in 2010. This is a 2.5% increase over 2009 sales. Restaurant industry sales account for 4% of the GNP for the United States.

Approximately 48% of all food dollars spent by consumers is spent in eating and drinking establishments. That figure is up dramatically since 1955 in which only 25% of all consumers spending for food and drink when to restaurants. A total of 43% of adults believe that eating away is as cost effective as cooking at home and cleaning up. Time is money.

The baby boomer population, the demographic segment that has the most significant impact in terms of marketing and menu mix, is getting older. In the coming years, over 20% of the population will be between the ages of 50 and 64.The dining habits of this important demographic group will influence menus and restaurant concepts into the future. Mikhail's Tacos will keep up with these trends.

Households with income before taxes of $30,000 or more spend more on dining out. Household incomes of greater than $75,000 have increased to almost one quarter of all meals consumed outside the home. As one might imagine, higher income households tend to spend more of their food dollars in meals away from home.

The National Restaurant Association's most recent survey on restaurant spending found that the typical American household spent $2,634 on food away from home. Households in metropolitan areas tend to spend more than households in rural areas. Households with income over $70,000 spent an average of $4,544 on food away from home. The report also showed that adults between 35 and 54 spend more on food away from home as a result of their higher incomes, averaging $3,234 for meals outside the home.

The report discussed beverages and noted the continuing popularity of bottled water, coffee and espresso drinks, iced tea, and increasing wine sales at full service restaurants. Mikhail's will offer a full service bar to take advantage of these trends. However, it will offer a brewed Latin coffee but will not venture into espresso drinks.

Greater use of technology and more reliance on staff training will be used to increase productivity and gain higher revenues. More than two-thirds of restaurant operators say they are more productive than they were two years ago. Over twenty five percent of food-service operators say they are increasing their budget for technology spending.

Over sixty percent of all restaurants now have websites. In addition to posting information such as menu, nutrition and location, an increasing number are expected to offer other services such as reservations, delivery and takeout ordering.

Gift cards and gift certificates in restaurants continue to be the number one preference by consumers as compared to other retail industries. Gift card and gift certificate sales account for roughly 5% of annual restaurant sales. Mikhail's will offer gift cards from day one.

For more information about current trends and statistics, visit the National Restaurant Association website at www.restaurant.org.

Marketing Strategies

Advertising strategies include local TV advertisements to initially announce the Grand Opening. Print advertisements will run in the local newspaper, campus newspaper, lifestyle magazine, and the local events calendar. The first two times these print ads run, they will include a coupon for a discounted menu item.

Promotional strategies will focus on notifying the campus and nearby businesses that we are open and will appeal to their needs. Alexei is adept at social networking strategies and Facebook, Twitter and other sites will be used to promote the restaurant. Coupons and take-out menus will be included in the packets students receive when they move into the dorms and register for classes. Take-out menus and coupons will also be distributed to the surrounding business offices.

PR also will include the distribution of press releases to local media focusing on the human-interest story behind the restaurant. The goal is to get a profile of Mikhail and Alexei into the local papers and onto the radio. This unique story of Russian immigrants specializing in Mexican food in America is bound to attract interested customers.

Mikhail's Tacos will aggressively seek to build a database of our guests. Guests will have an opportunity to be included in the database so they can participate in our promotions such as birthday or anniversary cards and frequent diner program.

The restaurant's marketing plan will include an active Frequent Diner program. The program will allow us to reward out guests for their continued patronage. The program shall have flexibility to allow us to be creative in our reward structure. Additionally, it should allow us to adapt to changing market trends.

We anticipate capitalizing on our customer database by instituting an effective email marketing strategy. We will give our customer the option to receive email communications from our restaurant. Customer's privacy will be protected and we will not email our customers without their permission.

Our email marketing strategy will include an awareness not to inundate our guests with email. Promotional content will be developed with the goal of enticement versus quantity. The program will incorporate tools to measure effectiveness and customer satisfaction.

Two main marketing strategies have been developed at this time. The first is to emphasize the freshness and flavor of the gourmet food that features adventurous ingredients. Food will be prepared quickly and is reasonably priced. This message will be directed toward surrounding business people looking for a quick and healthy lunch, and to students looking for great food that won't empty their pockets. Food will be served in a fun and friendly environment and will also be available for take-out.

The second strategy focuses on the Russian brothers that have mastered (and reinvented) Mexican cuisine for Americans. Formerly bike mechanics, they are ready to bring their new take on tacos and burritos to their own restaurant. It is an only-in-America story that will resonate will throughout Northern Nevada and beyond.

Customer Service

Customer Service at Mikhail's Tacos will be given special emphasis. It is estimated that only 1 in 22 customers who have a problem in a restaurant will tell management about it. Mikhail's Tacos shall engage in responsive and proactive customer service.

All guest complaints will be acknowledged by the staff and immediately referred to management. Programs will be in place to promptly deal with various types of guest complaints. More serious complaints will be documented and kept on file.

Training programs will include specific material to teach our employees about service attitudes, customer perception and how to deal with guest complaints. Management will conduct periodic staff meetings intended to review policy, increase guest satisfaction and to keep a general line of communication between staff and management.

V. Financials

The start-up costs for Mikhail's Tacos, Inc. will be approximately $100,000, and includes leasehold improvements, permits, inventory, and working capital requirements. Start-up costs will be financed by shareholder investments.

Use of Funds

Capital Expenditures

Leasehold Improvements	30,000
Equipment and Furniture	15,000
Total Capital Expenditures	**45,000**

Working Capital

Rent (four months)	12,000
Salaries	10,000
Start-Up Inventory	8,000
Legal	2,000
Permits and Licenses	2,500
Printing	2,000
Graphic Design	1,000
Insurance	2,500
Working Capital Reserve	15,000
Total Working Capital	**55,000**

Total Use of Funds   **100,000**

Sources of Funds

Mikhail Ramnikov	25,000
Alexei Ramnikov	25,000
Shareholder Investments	<u>50,000</u>
Total Sources of Funds	**100,000**

Projected Income Statement – Mikhail's Tacos, Inc.

	Year One	Year Two	Year Three
Income			
Gross Sales	540,000	630,000	792,000
less returns and allowances	0	0	0
Net Sales	540,000	630,000	792,000
Cost of Sales	189,000	220,500	285,120
Gross Profit	351,000	409,500	506,880
Gross Profit Margin	65%	65%	64%
Operating Expenses			
General and Administrative Expenses			
Salaries and Wages	196,000	215,600	237,160
Employee Benefits	20,000	22,000	24,200
Payroll Taxes	15,000	16,500	18,150
Professional Services	2,500	2,700	2,900
Rent	36,000	37,800	39,690
Maintenance	2,000	2,200	2,400
Equipment Rental	1,000	1,100	1,200
Equipment and Furniture Purchase	2,200	2,500	2,900
Marketing and Advertising	24,000	26,000	28,000
Utilities	2,100	2,250	2,375
Insurance	1,200	1,400	1,600
Office Supplies	800	900	1000
Postage	500	550	600
Entertainment	2,500	3,000	3,500
Travel	300	350	400
Bad Debt	100	150	200
Depreciation and Amortization	2,200	2,500	2,800
Total Operating Expenses	**308,400**	**337,500**	**369,075**
Net Income Before Taxes	**42,600**	**72,000**	**137,805**
Taxes on Income (35%)	**14,910**	**25,200**	**48,232**
Net Income After Taxes	**27,690**	**46,800**	**89,573**

Projected Balance Sheet

	Year 1	Year 2	Year 3
Current Assets			
Cash	85,390	134,190	226,063
Accounts receivable	1,000	1,500	2,000
Inventory	500	750	1,000
Total Current Assets	86,890	136,440	229,063
Non-Current Assets			
Fixed assets-leasehold improvements	47,200	49,700	52,600
Accumulated depreciation	(2,200)	(4,700)	(7,500)
Total Non-Current Assets	45,000	45,000	45,100
Total Assets	131,890	181,440	274,163
Current liabilities			
Accounts payable	2,000	2,250	2,500
Non-Current Assets			
Notes Payable	-	-	-
Stockholder's Equity			
Contributed Capital	100,000	100,000	100,000
Retained Earnings	29,890	79,190	171,663
Total Stockholder's Equity	129,890	179,190	271,663
Total Liabilities and Stockholder's Equity	131,890	181,440	274,163

Projected Statement of Cash Flows

	Year 1	Year 2	Year 3
Income from Operations	29,890	49,300	92,473
Changes in depreciation	2,200	2,500	2,800
Changes in inventory	(500)	(250)	(250)
Changes in receivables	(1,000)	(500)	(500)
Changes in payables	2,000	250	250
Net cash provided by operations	32,590	51,300	94,773
Cash used in investing activities			
Purchases of fixed assets	(47,200)	(2,500)	(2,900)
Cash from financing activities			
Proceeds from issuance of stock	100,000	-	-
Changes in cash position	85,390	48,800	91,873
Beginning cash	-	85,390	134,190
Ending cash balance	85,390	134,190	226,063

Break Even Analysis

	Year 1	Year 2	Year 3
Net sales	540,000	630,000	792,000
Cost of Goods sold	189,000	220,500	285,120
Gross profit	351,000	409,500	506,880
Gross profit percentage	65.00%	65.00%	64.00%
Total Operating Expenses *	308,400	337,500	369,075
Divided by Gross Profit Margin Percentage	65.00%	65.00%	64.00%
Break Even Sales	474,462	519,231	576,680

* This amount includes payroll which can fluctuate depending on the level of sales.

Average price per meal	$ 6.50	$ 6.50	$ 6.50
Break Even Meals	72,994	79,882	88,720
Divided by # days	365	365	365
Number of meals per day required to break even	200	219	243

VI. Supporting Documents

Management

Mikhail's Tacos, Inc. will utilize the respective strengths of its management, combining business experience with years of training in food preparation.

Mikhail Ramnikov, President

Mikhail Ramnikov received a degree in business from his university in Moscow while also serving as an assistant manager in his father's grocery store. After achieving his degree, he started his own bicycle supply and repair shop from the ground up. For twelve years, he ran every aspect of the small business, from advertising to bookkeeping, from ordering to quality control. He managed a small team of skilled repairmen but did much of the sales himself. The shop was one of the most well-respected small businesses in the area. When Mikhail decided to move to America, he sold the business for a profit.

While Mikhail has always had a mind for business, he has always loved to cook. Since his days in his father's grocery store, he has always experimented with different flavors and recipes. He realized that this was his true passion and wanted to combine his business sense with his love of cooking.

Although he does not have prior experience in the food service industry, his business experience and success will carry over into this venture. He will act as president of Mikhail's Tacos, Inc., and will serve on the Board of Directors.

Alexei Ramnikov, Secretary and Treasurer

Alexei's love of food was born when he worked in his father's grocery store. He decided to pursue this love further by attending a respected culinary school in Moscow. Straight out of school, he was hired to work at the restaurant in the four-star Hotel Sieyna in Moscow. He worked there for fifteen years, growing under the instruction of some of the best chefs in the country, until he was appointed head chef at the restaurant.

After leaving Moscow, he landed a head chef position in a gourmet bistro in Los Angeles. His work at Le Bistro was featured in numerous trade magazines and attracted a group of loyal patrons. However, his desire to head his own kitchen in a partnership with his brother brought him to Reno. He will serve as secretary and treasurer for Mikhail's Tacos, Inc., and will also serve on the Board of Directors.

Restaurant Industry Trends

Sales in the restaurant industry are expected to increase by 3.6 percent this year after three years of negative growth. In the specific area of fast casual dining, sales have increased 8% since 2006. Fast-food chains' popularity seems to be slipping, with only 3 percent of Americans eating at a fast-food chain every week. Restaurants with seated dining and full service by a waiter or waitress make up over half of all U.S. restaurant sales. It is estimated that restaurant sales will_reach a record 604 billion dollars this year.

Fast casual restaurants, typically individually owned establishments, have become popular. They combine fast delivery of food with a casual but often full-service environment. Many of these restaurants do not have full bar service, which Mikhail's Tacos, Inc. will be offering.

Fast casual restaurants characteristically offer fresh ingredients rather than mostly fried foods. Many specialize in sandwiches or wraps and do a majority of their business during their lunch service. Most products are made to order, lessening the use of frozen ingredients. Foods contain a variety of interesting flavors and ingredients, offering the patron an extensive selection of menu items. They also offer the increasingly popular service of takeout meals. Examples of national chain fast casual restaurants are Pick Up Stix, Baja Fresh, Chipotle Grill, and Panera Bread.

Pricing at this type of establishment is more than the bargain fast-food pricing but less than the menu prices at a regular restaurant. Typically, the average cost per menu item is under $10. For this price, people are expecting more: good service, consistent taste, and a pleasing atmosphere.

There have been notable trends established among those who eat out. More young adults dine out than older adults. Diners aged eighteen to forty-four dine outside the home nearly twice as many times per week as those over sixty-five years of age.

Many of these diners are considered adventurous diners. They are usually well educated and enjoy trying new restaurants, usually individually owned ones. They consciously steer away from chain restaurants. They are considered adventurous because they move away from established brands and chains to try more creative foods, including ethnic cuisines.

Health consciousness among diners has become a popular trend. Restaurants have had to respond accordingly, offering foods with lowered calorie, fat, or carbohydrate content to meet the consumer demand for such items. Vegetarian items have become common. Some restaurants highlight the more healthful items they offer, and some even offer nutritional breakdowns of dishes on their menus. A total of 71% of adults said they are trying to eat healthier at restaurants than they did two years ago.

Local Trends

Reno, Nevada, is the largest and leading city within the growing northern Nevada region. Located within a short drive of the skiing and outdoor recreation area of Lake Tahoe, Reno is a city on the rise. In 2011, there were 219,636 residents, a number that is expected to rise to 263,269 by 2025, according to the City of Reno.

Reno is home to the University of Nevada, Reno, an institution with nearly 20,000 students, a number expected to increase rapidly in the coming years. The school was recently rated one of the top national universities by *U.S. News and World Report*.

The business community in Reno is vibrant and resilient. The Reno area has attracted well-known businesses such as Barnes & Noble, Intuit, Microsoft Licensing, and Amazon. The business community is now garnering national media attention. Reno's national recognition includes the following:

- One of the Twenty Five Best Places to Live in 2010
  Men's Journal Magazine

- Nevada #5 on the Seven Best States to Start a Business
  US News and World Report

- Best Small City in America for Small Business
  Dun & Bradstreet; Entrepreneur Magazine

- Ten Best Places to Live
  Cities Ranked and Rated

- Top Three Booming Towns
  Fortune

- One of the top cities for quality of life and
  a business-friendly atmosphere
  Time

- #8 in the 50 Best Small Cities to Live In
  Men's Journal

- #25 in the 150 Best Places for Business
  Forbes

Tourism continues to bring thousands of people to the area each year. The Reno/Tahoe International Airport reports that about 10,500 passengers arrive and depart the airport every day.

A thriving arts and cultural district located downtown and not far from the proposed restaurant location near the university attracts people with its galleries, coffee shops, the Nevada Museum of Art, the Reno Aces ballpark, a Triple A baseball stadium, and the new Discovery Museum.

Visitors come to the area to take advantage of a wide range of recreational opportunities, including skiing and water sports, kayaking at the new white-water park on the river, hiking, camping, and fishing. Nightlife and entertainment attract many visitors as well.

The continued growth of the area combined with tourism and a dynamic business community amounts to promising demographics for Mikhail's Tacos, Inc.

Index

How Can I Protect My Personal, Business and Real Estate Assets?

For information on forming corporations, limited liability companies
and limited partnerships to protect your personal, business and real
estate holdings in all 50 states visit the Corporate Direct website at

www.CorporateDirect.com

or

call toll-free: 1-800-600-1760

Mention this book and receive a discount on your basic formation fee.

About the Author

Garrett Sutton, Esq., is the bestselling author of *Start Your Own Corporation, Run Your Own Corporation, The ABC's of Getting Out of Debt, Writing Winning Business Plans, Buying and Selling a Business* and *The Loopholes of Real Estate* in Robert Kiyosaki's Rich Dad's Advisors series. Garrett has over thirty years experience in assisting individuals and business to determine their appropriate corporate structure, limit their liability, protect their assets and advance their financial, personal and credit success goals.

Garrett and his law firm, Sutton Law Center, have offices in Reno, Nevada, Jackson Hole, Wyoming and Sacramento, California. The firm represents clients in their real estate and business-related law matters.

Garrett is also the owner of Corporate Direct, which since 1988 has provided affordable asset protection and corporate formation services. He is the author of *How to Use Limited Liability Companies and Limited Partnerships,* published by Success DNA, which further educates readers on the proper use of entities. Along with credit expert Gerri Detweiler, Garrett also assists entrepreneurs build business credit. Please see businesscreditsuccess.com for more information.

Garrett attended Colorado College and the University of California at Berkeley, where he received a B.S. in Business Administration in 1975. He graduated with a J.D. in 1978 from Hastings College of Law, the University of California's law school in San Francisco. Garrett is a member of the State Bar of Nevada, the State Bar of California, and the American Bar Association.

For more information on Garrett Sutton and Sutton Law Center, please visit his Web sites at www.sutlaw.com, www.corporatedirect.com, www.businesscreditsuccess.com and www.successdna.com.

Other Books by
Garrett Sutton, Esq.

Start Your Own Corporation
Why the Rich Own their Own Companies and Everyone Else Works for Them

Writing Winning Business Plans
How to Prepare a Business Plan that Investors Will Want to Read – and Invest In

Buying and Selling a Business
How You Can Win in the Business Quadrant

The ABCs of Getting Out of Debt
Turn Bad Debt into Good Debt and Bad Credit into Good Credit

Run Your Own Corporation
How to Legally Operate and Properly Maintain Your Company into the Future

The Loopholes of Real Estate
Secrets of Successful Real Estate Investing

• • • • • • • • • • •

How to Use Limited Liability Companies & Limited Partnerships
Getting the Most Out of Your Legal Structure
(a SuccessDNA book)

Bulletproof Your Corporation, Limited Liability Company and Limited Partnership
How to Raise and Maintain the Corporate Veil of Protection
(a Corporate Direct book)

Start a Business Toolbox
A Complete Resource for New Entrepreneurs
(a Corporate Direct book)